THE
HISTORY OF
AGRICULTURE

FOOD AND SOCIETY

THE HISTORY OF AGRICULTURE

Edited by Gini Gorlinski, Associate Editor, Arts and Culture

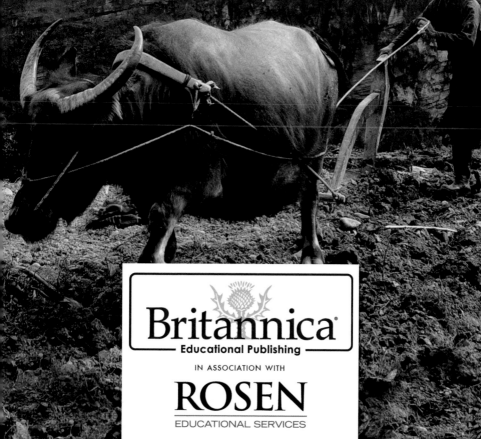

Britannica
Educational Publishing

IN ASSOCIATION WITH

ROSEN
EDUCATIONAL SERVICES

Published in 2013 by Britannica Educational Publishing
(a trademark of Encyclopædia Britannica, Inc.)
in association with Rosen Educational Services, LLC
29 East 21st Street, New York, NY 10010.

Distributed exclusively by Rosen Educational Services.
For a listing of additional Britannica Educational Publishing titles, call toll free (800) 237-9932.

First Edition

Britannica Educational Publishing
J.E. Luebering: Senior Manager
Adam Augustyn, Assistant Manager
Marilyn L. Barton: Senior Coordinator, Production Control
Steven Bosco: Director, Editorial Technologies
Lisa S. Braucher: Senior Producer and Data Editor
Yvette Charboneau: Senior Copy Editor
Kathy Nakamura: Manager, Media Acquisition
Gini Gorlinski: Associate Editor, Arts and Culture

Rosen Educational Services
Shalini Saxena: Editor
Nelson Sá: Art Director
Cindy Reiman: Photography Manager
Brian Garvey: Designer, Cover Design
Introduction by Gini Gorlinski

Library of Congress Cataloging-in-Publication Data

The history of agriculture/edited by: Gini Gorlinski.—1st ed.
    p. cm.—(Food and society)
"In association with Britannica Educational Publishing, Rosen Educational Services."
Includes bibliographical references and index.
ISBN 978-1-61530-919-1 (library binding)
 1. Agriculture—History. I. Gorlinski, Gini. II. Series: Food and society.
S419.H5697 2012
630.9—dc23

                                                               2012015731

Manufactured in the United States of America

On the cover, p.iii: A Hmong woman turns the earth in the Vietnamese province of Hà Giang, where the economy is largely based on agriculture. Both centuries-old agricultural techniques and new technological developments can be seen throughout the world today. *Hoang Dinh Nam/AFP/Getty Images*

xiii

12

37

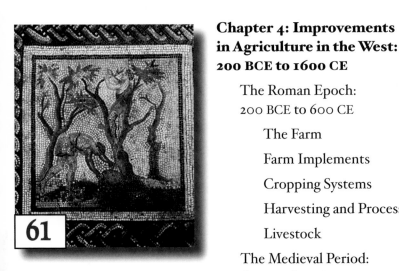

78

81

91

95

104

Chapter 7: The 20th Century: New Machines, Crops, and Farming Techniques 101

109

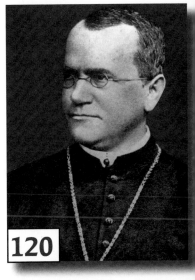

120

131

INTRODUCTION

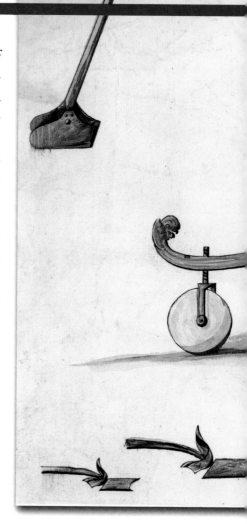

Agriculture is a form of environmental engineering that has for millennia been an occupation—and pre-occupation—of humankind. Grasses and grains have been cultivated for convenient consumption for nearly 12,000 years, while service animals, most notably dogs, have worked alongside for an even longer period. Such domestication of plants and animals to meet the ever-increasing needs of humankind was the initial impetus for the agricultural endeavour, and, indeed, it continues to drive the industry today.

How is it possible to know about agriculture to such historical depth, when written records of agricultural activities go back only about 5,000 years? Is scholarship necessarily limited to mere speculation? Not at all. Application of certain scientific techniques and methodologies has enabled the construction of a credible and thorough account of the advent, development, dissemination, and diversity of agricultural activity across the globe.

An illustration of a seed drill designed by British agricultural-ist and inventor Jethro Tull. Although Tull did not invent the seed drill, his design mechanized the process of planting seeds more efficiently than prior attempts, and by the end of the 18th century, numerous other inventors had followed suit.
Time & Life Pictures/Getty Images

Among the most important data-generating devices available to researchers of ancient agriculture has been the process of carbon-14 dating, developed in 1949 by American physicist Willard F. Libby. Carbon-14 dating is a method of estimating the age of organic materials based on their carbon-14, or radiocarbon, content. Radiocarbon is an element that is always present in the atmosphere. It is absorbed from the air by green plants, from plants by the animals that eat them, and from other animals by carnivorous organisms. Ultimately, the level of radiocarbon present in living plants and animals is equal to that present in the atmosphere. Once an organism dies, however, it no longer absorbs radiocarbon. Rather, the element begins to decay to nitrogen, very slowly but at a steady pace, with a "half-life" of 5,730 plus or minus 40 years. This means that after about 5,730 years, only half of the radiocarbon present in a plant or animal at its time of death will remain. Because the element decays at such a regular rate, it is possible for scientists to measure the level of residual radiocarbon in bones, fossils, or other organic matter, then to compare that to the level of radiocarbon in the atmosphere, and, finally, to calculate with reasonable precision how long it has been since a plant or animal died. As an effective means of determining the age of organic matter—such as charred remains of plants and animals in an ancient hearth—between 500 and 50,000 years old, carbon-14 dating indeed has been an indispensable tool in the ongoing quest to grasp the early history of agriculture in human society.

Other means by which scientists are able to ascertain the nature of early agriculture and plant domestication include the analysis of certain plant remains known as phytoliths, starch granules, and pollen grains. Phytoliths are microscopic silica (quartzlike) particles produced in the cells of many plants to help reinforce the plants' physical structure. After a plant dies or is destroyed, the phytoliths remain, retaining for long periods the shape of the cells in which they were formed. Similarly, the remains of starch and pollen grains, both products of green plants, are highly resistant to decay and may be preserved for centuries in sediments long after their parent plants are gone. The shapes of plant cells (recorded in phytoliths), starch granules, and pollen grains are often unique to a specific type of plant. Consequently, they provide "fingerprints" that can be lifted from the surfaces of cooking pots and assorted tools at ancient archaeological sites. By studying such plant residue—such as corn phytoliths on an ancient South American ceramic vessel—scientists have been able to determine what sorts of plants were consumed, cultivated, and, ultimately, domesticated in different areas worldwide.

Technically, a plant or animal is domesticated when it becomes reliant on human care for its long-term survival and proliferation. When people domesticate plants or animals in any significant quantity, they typically engineer the land in some respect to accommodate their crops and livestock. Clearing the land of trees and undergrowth brings more light into the growing area. Tilling the soil as well as weeding helps to reduce competition with disruptive plants and other unwanted organisms. Weak or marginal soils may be enriched with organic fertilizers (e.g., manure) or synthetic substances to promote healthy crops that bear an abundance of fruit. A single field may also be planted over the course of several years with a specific sequence—or rotation—of crops that alternately sap and restore the soil's nutrients. As part of the rotation, some fields may lie fallow, or uncultivated, for a given period in order to regain their fertility and, in some cases, to provide grazing ground for livestock.

In addition to clearing, fertilizing, and selectively cultivating land for optimal agricultural yield, cultures around the world have developed an array of ingenious irrigation strategies to ensure that their farms receive an adequate and appropriate amount of water. Archaeological evidence as well as contemporary practice has indicated that the first irrigation systems were likely devised by the ancient Egyptians in the Nile River valley. Every year, the river floods naturally, inundating the surrounding plains. In anticipation of the flood, ancient farmers built earth barriers to direct the flood waters to particular areas, or basins. Water was retained in the basins, and the Nile's nutrient-rich silts were allowed to settle for some time after the river proper had receded. When the basins were finally drained, moist, fertile farmland was left behind, sufficient to sustain healthy crop growth from germination to harvest. Such basin irrigation was widely practiced in the Nile valley until well into the 20th century, when it was superseded by perennial irrigation, a system that uses dams to store larger amounts of water for strategic year-round release to farmlands throughout the region. Unlike basin irrigation, which permits just one harvest annually, perennial irrigation enables the harvest of multiple crops in a single year. Perennial irrigation also serves to minimize disruption of agricultural activities in times of drought.

While the flood plains such as those of the Nile River have presented one set of agricultural challenges, rugged terrain in other parts of the world have posed yet another. In many areas, fertile soils are available only on the slopes of hills and mountains. The steep grade of the land, however, limits retention of water at higher elevations, because the water constantly seeks lower ground. As the water flows downward, it carries soil with it, ultimately eroding away valuable farmland. In response to such conditions, many societies have irrigated hilly regions by sculpting the slopes into terraces, which allows regulation of the flow of water to all levels while simultaneously controlling erosion. In South America, such terracing was practiced by the 15th-century Inca in what is now Peru. Evidence of similar water management also exists in Mesoamerica and many other parts of the world. Indeed, terraced cultivation continues to characterize many agricultural societies today. No image of Bali, Indo., for instance, would be complete without an account or snapshot of the shimmering rice fields hugging the hills of the island's interior.

Environmental engineering in the form of land and water management constitutes just one part of the agricultural enterprise. For centuries, plants and animals also have been subject to calculated alteration, and domestication itself brought about significant changes in these organisms. Seeds, fruit, and tubers became bigger, while animals typically produced more meat, milk, or wool. Domestication also made animals relatively docile, rendering them more useful in a service capacity. Both farmers and scientists have experimented with crossbreeding in an effort to isolate and amplify these and other desirable characteristics in their crops and livestock. In the early 19th century, for instance, a farmer in Pennsylvania realized that the crossbreeding of a hard-kerneled, early-maturing type of corn (maize) with a soft-kerneled, late-maturing, higher yielding variety produced a new, hardier strain that embodied the best characteristics of both parent species. Work in this area accelerated after the publication of Austrian monk and botanist Gregor Mendel's pioneering research in plant genetics in the mid-19th century. Genetic engineering gained momentum in the early 1900s and by mid-century, almost all cornfields in the U.S. Midwest were planted with hybrid seed. Wheat and rice were also heavily hybridized in the 20th century, with new strains developed to thrive in particular climatic conditions in North America, Mesoamerica, Asia, and elsewhere.

Animals have been hybridized somewhat less aggressively than crops, but crossbreeding has nevertheless played a central role in the improvement of livestock. By nearly 5,000 years ago, Egyptians were already practicing specialized breeding of cattle and sheep, some for meat, others for milk. By the 18th century Europeans had similarly recognized the advantages of careful crossbreeding in elevating the quality of their farm animals. By the early 20th century the same sorts of revelations in genetics that propelled plant hybridization were contributing to the customization of many breeds of livestock to suit specific regional tastes and values. In New Zealand, sheep were bred primarily for their meat, while in the United States they were engineered not only to produce abundant wool and meat but also to endure harsh climates of the western rangelands. American farmers also engineered pigs to produce more lard, but when the demand for lard later decreased, a leaner breed was developed. Meanwhile, cattle from India were crossbred with North American species to yield animals that were more resistant to the heat and insects of the American South and Southwest.

No history of agriculture is complete without addressing the peripherals—the tools and machinery—that have been indispensable to farmers through the ages. From the first efforts at cultivation to the most recent innovations in genetic engineering, increasingly sophisticated technologies have been employed in working the soil, planting and harvesting crops, and raising and processing livestock and their products. Archaeological records indicate that oxen-drawn wooden plows without wheels were used some five millennia ago by Sumerians and Egyptians to break up the topsoil in preparation for sowing barley and wheat. By the 10th century western European farmers employed wheeled plows that not only tilled the land but also turned it over, making the soil more suitable for seeding. Use of a hand-held dibble stick to punch holes into the ground to receive seeds is among the oldest methods of sowing. Also ancient is the practice of attaching to the plow a seed drill, a device that places and covers the seeds with soil immediately after the ground is tilled, thereby collapsing the tasks of tilling and sowing into a single operation. By at least the early 17th century, drill sowing of rice, millet, and wheat was widespread in India.

Such combination of multiple activities into a single process has been an ongoing trend in most areas of the world since the advent of agriculture. Developments in machinery for grain production offer a case in point. The harvesting of grain generally consists of three basic components: picking the crop; removing the grain from the stalk (threshing); and removing the chaff from the grain (winnowing). In the earliest days of agriculture, grain was usually cut by hand, threshed under the hooves of cattle, and winnowed by the wind. By the mid-20th century the tractor-drawn grain combine—one machine that accomplished all three tasks—was widely used on larger farms in the United States. Other sorts of dedicated equipment were designed for the harvest of corn, cotton, and tomatoes, among other crops. Parallel strides were made in the meat and dairy industries, as multi-tasking machines accomplished more quickly, easily, and inexpensively most of the work that was formerly performed manually.

Agriculture is a multifaceted, ever-expanding, and increasingly sophisticated phenomenon. The aim of this volume is to chart, albeit briefly, the development of the industry from its earliest manifestations, as chronicled in the organic remains of ancient settlements, to its 21st-century presence as a meticulously documented, high-tech global enterprise. With its frequently shifting focus, the narrative also intends to illuminate the many ways in which agricultural experiences and techniques have varied across geographic, temporal, cultural, and national boundaries. By the time readers reach the final pages of text, they will have a grasp not only of the diversity of land- and water-management systems but also of the domestication, dissemination, and engineering of highly productive plant and animal species over time. Moreover, they will have a sense of the myriad technologies, both positive and negative, that have accompanied agriculture at every turn. Ultimately, readers will recognize agriculture as a remarkable testament to the resourcefulness, ingenuity, and interconnectedness of humankind.

CHAPTER 1

HOW AGRICULTURE AND DOMESTICATION BEGAN

Agriculture has no single, simple origin. A wide variety of plants and animals have been independently domesticated at different times and in numerous places. The first agriculture appears to have developed at the closing of the last Pleistocene glacial period, or Ice Age (about 11,700 years ago). At that time temperatures warmed, glaciers melted, sea levels rose, and ecosystems throughout the world reorganized. The changes were more dramatic in temperate regions than in the tropics.

Although global climate change played a role in the development of agriculture, it does not account for the complex and diverse cultural responses that ensued, the specific timing of the appearance of agricultural communities in different regions, or the specific regional impact of climate change on local environments. By studying populations that did not develop intensive agriculture or certain cultigens, such as wheat and rice, archaeologists narrow the search for causes. For instance, Australian Aborigines and many of the Native American peoples of western North America developed complex methods to manage diverse sets of plants and animals, often including (but not limited to) cultivation. These practices may be representative of activities common in some parts of the world more than 15,000 years ago.

Plant and animal management was and is a familiar concept within hunting and gathering cultures, but it

Painting of herdsmen and cattle, Tassili-n-Ajjer, Alg. 5000-1000 BCE. J.D. Lajoux

took on new dimensions as natural selection and mutation produced phenotypes (organisms that have adapted to their environments) that were increasingly reliant upon people. Because some resource management practices, such as intensively tending nondomesticated nut-bearing trees, bridge the boundary between foraging and farming, archaeologists investigating agricultural origins generally frame their work in terms of a continuum of subsistence practices.

Notably, agriculture does not appear to have developed in particularly impoverished settings; domestication does not seem to have been a response to food scarcity or deprivation. In fact, quite the opposite appears to be the case. It was once thought that human population pressure was a significant factor in the process, but by the late 20th century research indicated that populations rose significantly only after people had established food production.

Instead, it is thought that—at least initially—the new animals and plants that were developed through domestication may have helped to maintain ways of life that emphasized hunting and gathering by providing insurance in lean seasons. When considered in terms of food management, dogs may have been initially domesticated as hunting companions, while herds of sheep, goats, reindeer, or cattle may have been more reliable sources of meat and milk than their wild counterparts or other game animals. Domestication made resource planning a more predictable exercise in regions that combined extreme seasonal variation and rich natural resource abundance.

EARLIEST BEGINNINGS

The domestication of plants and animals caused changes in their form—the presence or absence of such changes indicates whether a given organism was wild or a domesticate. On the basis of such evidence, one of the oldest transitions from hunting and gathering to agriculture has been identified as dating to between 14,500 and 12,000 BP (before present) in Southwest Asia. It was experienced by groups known as Epipaleolithic peoples, who survived from the end of the Paleolithic Period into early post-glacial times and used smaller stone tools (microblades) than their predecessors. The Natufians, an Epipaleolithic culture located in the Levant (lands along the eastern Mediterranean shores), possessed stone sickles and intensively collected many plants, such as wild barley (*Hordeum spontaneum*). In the eastern Fertile Crescent of the Middle East, Epipaleolithic people who had been dependent on hunting gazelles (*Gazella* species), wild goats, and sheep began to raise goats and sheep, but not gazelles, as livestock. By 12,000–11,000 BP, and possibly earlier, domesticated forms of some plants had been developed in the region, and by 10,000 BP domesticated animals were appearing. Elsewhere in the Old World the archaeological record for the earliest agriculture is not as well known at this time, but by 8500–8000 BP millet (*Setaria italica* and *Panicum miliaceum*) and rice (*Oryza sativa*) were being domesticated in East Asia.

In the Americas, squash (*Cucurbita pepo* and *C. moschata*) existed in domesticated form in southern Mexico and northern Peru by about 10,000–9000 BP. By 5000–3000 BP the aboriginal peoples of eastern North America and what would become the southwestern United States were turning to agriculture. In sum, plant and animal domestication, and therefore agriculture, were undertaken in a variety of places, each independent of the others.

The dog appears to have been the earliest domesticated animal, as it is found in archaeological sites around the world by the end of the last glacial period. Genetic evidence indicates that a very small number of females—as few as three—were ancestral to 95 percent of all domesticated dogs. The species' greatest genetic diversity is in China, which indicates that the history of dogs is probably longer there than elsewhere. The earliest dogs found in the Americas are all descendants of the Chinese group, suggesting that they accompanied the first people to reach the New World, an event that occurred at least 13,000 years ago. People reached Beringia, the temporary land bridge between Siberia and Alaska, as long as 40,000 years ago, suggesting that dogs may have been domesticated even earlier.

Although the exact timing of dog domestication has not been definitively determined, it is clear that the dog was domesticated from the wolf. How and why this happened is not well understood, but the earliest dogs may have assisted humans with hunting and finding

BP VS. BCE VS. CE

The designation BP ("before present") appears after a date (e.g., 7000–5000 BP) that was determined through the carbon-14, or radiocarbon, dating process. Developed in the mid-1940s by scientist William F. Libby, carbon-14 dating relies on the measurement of a certain type of radioactive particle, carbon-14, that is present in the atmosphere and that is absorbed by all living plants and taken up by animals when they eat plants. After an organism dies, it no longer absorbs carbon-14; rather, the particles begin to decay at a regular, predictable rate. The regular decay of radiocarbon ultimately allows scientists to calculate about how long ago a given organism died by comparing the amount of carbon-14 remaining in the organism to the amount of carbon-14 in the atmosphere at "present." For ease of calculation, scientists fixed the "present" at 1950 in commemoration of the year in which the results of the first carbon-14 dating experiments were published.

Caution must be taken whenever attempting to convert BP dates to their BCE ("before the common era") or CE ("common era") equivalents. Because the concentration of carbon-14 in the atmosphere has changed somewhat over time, figures need to be calibrated to reflect conditions at the actual time of measurement. Such calibrated dates are indicated CALBP, meaning the number of years before 1950, and they may easily be converted to exact calendar years. Conversion to BCE or CE of uncalibrated BP dates are typically rendered as date ranges.

food. Studies have demonstrated that dogs as young as nine months of age are better at reading human social behaviour and communication than wolves or even chimpanzees. This characteristic appears to be inherited and would have established a very close bond between dogs and humans.

EARLY DEVELOPMENT

The development of agriculture involves an intensification of the processes used to extract resources from the environment: more food, medicine, fibre, and other resources can be obtained from a given area of land by encouraging useful plant and animal species and discouraging others. As the productivity and predictability of local resources increased, the logistics of their procurement changed, particularly regarding the extent to which people were prepared to travel in order to take advantage of seasonally available items. Group composition eventually became more stable, mobility declined, and, as a consequence, populations increased.

In terms of material culture, durable houses and heavy tools such as pestles, mortars, and grindstones, all of which had long been known, came into more general use. Although discussions of prehistoric cultures often imply a direct correlation between the development of pottery and the origins of agriculture, this is not a universal relationship. In some parts of the Old World, such as Southwest Asia, and in the Americas, pottery appears long after agriculture starts, while in East Asia, where the first pottery dates to as early as 13,700 BP, the opposite is the case.

SOUTHWEST ASIA

Village farming began to spread across Southwest Asia shortly after 10,000 BP, and in less than 1,000 years settled farming cultures were widespread in the region. Notably, the intensive harvesting of wild grains first appeared well before the Epipaleolithic Period. At the Ohalo II site in Israel (*c.* 23,000 BP), a small group of Upper Paleolithic people lived in brush shelters and harvested a wide range of grass seeds and other plant foods.

At the Netiv Hagdud site in Israel, dating to 11,500 BP, wild barley is the most common plant food found among the grass, legume, nut, and other plant remains. The Netiv Hagdud occupants manufactured and used large numbers of sickles, grinding tools, and storage facilities, indicating an agricultural lifeway that preceded domesticated plants. The barley at the site is wild in form, but the large quantities and singular importance of the plant indicate that it was a crop. Similarly, the cereals at the Syrian sites of Mureybet and Jerf el-Ahmar appear to be wild.

The Abū Hureyra site in Syria is the largest known site from the era when plants and animals were initially being domesticated. Two periods of occupation bracketing the transition to agriculture have been unearthed there. The people of the earlier, Epipaleolithic occupation lived in much the same manner as those at Netiv Hagdud. However, the wide array of plant and animal remains found at Abū Hureyra show that its residents were exploiting significant amounts of wild einkorn (the progenitor of domesticated wheat), rye (*Secale* species), and gazelle; in addition, they harvested lentils (*Lens* species) and vetch (*Vicia* species). The earliest rye at the site is directly radiocarbon-dated to 12,000 BP and may be domesticated. If so, it would be the earliest evidence of plant domestication in the world; however, the oldest indisputably domesticated grain is einkorn from Nevali Çori (Turkey) dating to about 10,500 BP.

During the later period of occupation, the people of Abū Hureyra grew a broader range of cultigens, including barley, rye, and two early forms of domesticated wheat: emmer (*Triticum turgidum dicoccun*) and einkorn (*Triticum monococcum*). Legumes, which fix nitrogen to the soil, were also grown; they helped to maintain soil health and added plant protein to the diet. In addition, a form of crop rotation came into use either by accident or by design, also helping to maintain soil fertility.

People in Southwest Asia had become dependent on cultigens by 10,000 BP, a rapid transition. The research at Abū Hureyra has suggested that the rapid development of farming in the region was caused by the sudden onset of a cool period, the Younger Dryas (c. 12,700–11,500 BP), during which most of the wild resources people had been using became scarce. This model suggests that agriculture was already a component of the economy and that it simply expanded to fill the gap left by this reduction in natural resources. This explanation may be too simplistic, or it may apply only to the Abū Hureyra region. At the time, people throughout Southwest Asia were developing agriculture in a variety of environments and using a diverse array of plants; they probably shifted to food production for different reasons depending on local conditions.

While village life and plant domestication were getting under way in the Fertile Crescent, people in the foothills of the Zagros Mountains (Iran) were relatively mobile, practicing vertical transhumance (seasonal migration of animals between lower and higher elevations). Wild goats and sheep were hunted at lower elevations in the colder months and at higher elevations in the warmer months. People also harvested wild grasses as they followed the animals. Sheep and goats eventually replaced gazelles as the primary animal food of Southwest Asia. The earliest evidence for managed sheep and goat herds, a decrease in the size of animals, is found at the Ganj Dareh (Ganj Darreh) site in Iran between about 10,500 and 10,000 BP. This size change may simply reflect an increase in the ratio of female to male animals, as these species are sexually dimorphic and many pastoral peoples preferentially consume male animals in order to preserve the maximum number of breeding females. The smaller size may also reflect the culling of large or aggressive males.

CROP ROTATION

Crop rotation is an agricultural system that involves the successive cultivation of different crops in a specified order on the same fields. It stands in contrast to the one-crop system or to haphazard crop successions.

Early experiments in crop rotation, such as those at the Rothamsted experimental station in England in the mid-19th century, pointed to the usefulness of selecting rotation crops from three classifications: cultivated row, close-growing grains, and sod-forming, or rest, crops. Such a classification provides a ratio basis for balancing crops in the interest of continuing soil protection and production economy. It is sufficiently flexible for adjusting crops to many situations, for making changes when needed, and for including go-between crops as cover and green manures.

A simple rotation would be one crop from each group with a 1:1:1 ratio. The first number in a rotation ratio refers to cultivated row crops, the second to close-growing grains, and the third to sod-forming, or rest, crops. Such a ratio signifies the need for three fields and three years to produce each crop annually. This requirement would be satisfied with a rotation of corn, oats, and clover or of potatoes, wheat, and clover-timothy, for example. Rotations for any number of fields and crop relationships can be described in this manner. In general, most rotations are confined to time limits of eight years or less.

In addition to the many beneficial effects on soils and crops, well-planned crop rotations also provide the business aspects of farming with advantages. Labour, power, and equipment can be handled with more efficiency; weather and market risks can be reduced; livestock requirements can be met more easily; and the farm can be a more effective year-round enterprise.

More than 1,000 years later, the Ali Kosh site (also in Iran) was settled. This site is located in a lower elevation zone than Ganj Dareh, outside the natural range of goats. Goat remains at Ali Kosh show clear signs of domestication—the females have no horns. Sheep and goats were herded at Abū Hureyra by 8000 BP. Cattle were not of immediate importance to the people of ancient Southwest Asia, although aurochs (*Bos primigenius*), the wild ancestors of modern cattle, were hunted throughout the region by about 10,000 BP and for the next 1,000 years diminished in body size. Smaller, domesticated forms of cattle were not prevalent until about 8000 BP in Anatolia and on the coast of the Mediterranean.

The successful agricultural system that would come to support Mesopotamia's complex forms of political organization began with the amalgamation, after 10,000 BP, of the predominantly grain-based economies found in the western Fertile Crescent and the livestock-based economies of the eastern Fertile Crescent to form a production system invested in both. During the earliest period of this transition, hoes or digging sticks were used to break the ground where necessary, and planting was probably accomplished by "treading in," a process in which livestock are made to plant seeds by walking over an area where they have been broadcast. Techniques of food storage grew in sophistication; there were pit silos and granaries, sometimes of quite substantial nature. In drier areas, crop irrigation, which greatly increased yield, was developed; with the increasing population, more labour was available to carry out wider irrigation projects

THE AMERICAS

Indigenous peoples in the Americas created a variety of agricultural systems that were suited to a wide range of environments, from southern Canada to southern South America and from high elevations in the Andes to the lowlands of the Amazon River. Agriculture arose independently in at least three regions: South America, Mesoamerica, and eastern North America. Although the Americas had several indigenous animal species that were domesticated, none were of an appropriate size or temperament for use as draft animals; as a result, the plow and other technology reliant on heavy traction were unknown.

Swidden production, also known as slash-and-burn agriculture, was practiced from temperate eastern North America to the tropical lowlands of South America. Field fertility in swidden systems resulted from the burning of trees and shrubs in order to add nutrients to the soil. Such systems had high ecological diversity, thus providing a range of resources and prolonging the usefulness of what would otherwise have been short-lived fields and gardens. Settlements moved when productivity significantly declined and firewood was in low supply.

Complex societies such as the Maya and Aztec used swidden agriculture to some extent, but elaborate irrigation systems and tropical ecosystem management techniques were necessary to support their dense populations. In Peru the Inca built terraced fields on the steep Andean slopes. Foot plows and hoes were used to prepare these fields. Llama and alpaca dung, as well as human waste, provided fertilizer. Such fields were not limited to the Incas, however; terraced fields were also constructed in northern Mexico.

Corn, or maize (*Zea mays*), was the most widely used crop in the Americas and was grown nearly everywhere there was food production. Other crops had more-limited distributions. Important cultigens native to the Americas included potato, squash, amaranth (*Amaranthus species*), avocado (*Persea americana*), common bean (*Phaseolus vulgaris*), scarlet

Terraced fields near Arequipa in the southern Andes region of Peru. Chip and Rosa Maria de la Cueva Peterson

runner bean (*Phaseolus coccineus*), tepary bean (*Phaseolus acutifolius*), lima bean (*Phaseolus lunatus*), cacao (*Theobroma cacao*), coca (*Erythroxylon coca*), manioc (cassava; *Manihot esculenta*), papaya (*Carica candicans*), peanuts (groundnuts; *Arachis hypogea*), quinoa (*Chenopodium quinoa*), huazontle (*Chenopodium nutalliae*), pepper (*Capsicum* species), two types of cotton (*Gossypium hirsutum* and *G. barbadense*), pineapple (*Ananus comosus*), tomato (*Lycopersicon esculentum*), tobacco (*Nicotiana* species), sweet potato (*Ipomea batatus*), and sunflower (*Helianthus annuus*). Animals domesticated in the Americas included the alpaca (*Lama pacos*), llama (*Lama glama*), *cavi*, or guinea pig (*Cavia porcellus*), Muscovy duck (*Cairina moschata*), and turkey (*Meleagris gallopavo*).

TERRACE CULTIVATION

Terrace cultivation is a method of growing crops on the sides of hills or mountains by planting on graduated terraces built into the slope. Though labour-intensive, the method has been employed effectively to maximize arable land area in variable terrains and to reduce soil erosion and water loss.

In most systems the terrace is a low, flat ridge of earth built across the slope, with a channel for runoff water just above the ridge. Usually terraces are built on a slight grade so that the water caught in the channel moves slowly toward the terrace outlet. In areas where soils are able to take in water readily and rainfall is relatively low, level terraces may be used.

Terrace cultivation has been practiced in China, Japan, the Philippines, and other areas of Oceania and Southeast Asia; around the Mediterranean; in parts of Africa; and in the Andes of South America for centuries.

Terraced rice paddies near Bandarawela, Sri Lanka. © Robert Frerck/Stone

The earliest evidence of crops appears between 9000 and 8000 BP in Mexico and South America. The first crops in eastern North America may be almost as old, but substantial evidence for crop use there begins between 5000 and 4000 BP. Corn, the crop that eventually dominated most of the agricultural systems in the New World, appears rather suddenly in Mexico between 6300 and 6000 BP but was clearly domesticated earlier than that. Indigenous peoples in the Americas domesticated fewer animal species than their Old World counterparts, in large part because the Americas were home to fewer gregarious, or herding, species of appropriate size and temperament. Substantial villages were built only after the development of most crops; this contrasts with Old World practices, in which settled villages and towns appear to have developed earlier than, or at the same time as, agriculture.

EAST ASIA

Farming communities arose sometime before 8000 BP in China, but how much earlier is not yet known. In general, people in northern China domesticated foxtail and broomcorn millets (*Setaria italica* and *Panicum miliaceum*), hemp (*Cannabis sativa*), and Chinese cabbage (*Brassica campestris*), among other crops, while their contemporaries to the south domesticated rice. Water buffalo (*Bubalus bubalis*), swine, and chickens were also domesticated, but their earliest history is not yet documented in any detail.

Agricultural communities began to flourish between 8000 and 7000 BP in China, some relying on dry field production and others dependent on the annual rise and fall of water levels along the edges of rivers, lakes, and marshes in the Yangtze River (Chang Jiang) basin. The ingenious invention of paddy fields eventually came to mimic the natural wetland habitats favoured by rice and permitted the expansion and intensification of rice production.

People in the Korean peninsula and Japan eventually adopted rice and millet agriculture. They also raised crops not grown initially in China. A clearly domesticated soybean (*Glycine max*) was grown by 3000 BP in either northeast China or Korea. The adzuki, or red, bean (*Vigna angularis*) may have become a crop first in Korea, where considerable quantities of beans larger than their wild counterpart have been found in association with 3,000-year-old soybeans. Both types of beans have been recovered from earlier sites in China, but a sequence of development with which to document their domestication has yet to be established. Wild buckwheat (*Fagopyrum* species) is native to China, but archaeological evidence for the plant in East Asia is found only in Japan. Barnyard, or Japanese, millet (*Echinochloa esculenta* or *Echinochloa crusgalli utilis*) is known only in the archaeological record of Japan and is assumed to have been domesticated there.

EUROPE

In Europe agriculture developed through a combination of migration and diffusion. The oldest sites with agriculture are along the Mediterranean coast, where long-distance population movement and trade could be easily effected by boat. Franchthi Cave in southeastern Greece, a site occupied for more than 15,000 years, documents the development of agriculture in southern Europe over several centuries. A few Southwest Asian plants are part of the earlier record at Franchthi Cave, but there is no evidence that they were domesticated or cultivated. Wild emmer may have grown in the area at the time; it is not clear whether it was domesticated locally or had been brought in from Southwest Asia. The same may be true for lentils and grass peas (*Pisum* species). Shortly after 9000 BP sheep, goats, pigs, barley, lentils, and three types of wheat had become part of the resource base in the region. By 8000 BP cattle were added; at about the same time, crops and livestock were being introduced as far west as the Iberian Peninsula. Within five centuries, clear domesticates and a village-based agricultural way of life had been established on a coastal plain to the north at Nea Nikomedia (Macedonia).

As agriculture spread to more-temperate regions in Europe, practices that focused on cattle, pigs, emmer, einkorn, and legumes became important. In the milder and more arid regions along the Mediterranean coast, fewer modifications were necessary. When available, the incorporation of indigenous wild stock into domesticated herds doubtless aided animals' acclimatization, a practice that continued into historic times. The earliest evidence for agriculture northwest of the Black Sea comes from the Starčevo-Cris culture (*c.* 7500 BP), where four types of wheat, as well as oats (*Avena sativa*), barley, peas, and broomcorn millet, have been found. The millet is particularly interesting because it was extensively grown in northern China at the same time and presumably originated there, although it may have been independently domesticated in eastern Europe.

Agriculture spread through complex interactions between resident hunters and gatherers and agricultural peoples who were migrating into the region. The Linearbandkeramik, or LBK culture, is distributed widely across central Europe and is the first archaeological culture in the region for whom the material signature clearly demonstrates agriculture. However, it is unclear to what extent agriculture was spread through the exchange of ideas and to what extent it was spread via direct colonization. One study of the LBK culture, for instance, shows little change in the genetic makeup of local populations, an indication that ideas rather than people were moving across the landscape. As elsewhere, it is likely that new people and new ideas were accepted by established groups to varying degrees depending upon local conditions. For instance, in some areas, such as Hungary and Switzerland, many groups that adopted some form of agriculture also continued to rely upon hunting, sometimes retaining this practice for thousands of years.

However the expansion occurred, the archaeological signature of the LBK culture spread rapidly between 7300 and 6900 BP, moving westward at a rate of nearly 3 miles (5 km) per year. Archaeologists long presumed that LBK agriculture involved slash-and-burn techniques, in part because it was thought to be a necessary response to the region's low soil fertility and in part as an explanation for the culture's rapid expansion. However, experimental archaeology and plant remains from LBK sites have provided evidence that these people did not regularly shift their fields. By 6000 BP the transition to food production was under way in the British Isles, and by 5000 BP farming was common in western Europe.

CHAPTER 2

EARLY AGRICULTURAL SOCIETIES

In the Old World, settled life developed on the higher ground from Iran to Anatolia and the Levant and in China in the semiarid loess plains and the humid Yangtze valley. In contrast, the earliest civilizations based on complex and productive agriculture developed on the alluviums of the Tigris, Euphrates, and Nile rivers. Villages and townships existed in the Euphrates valley in the latter part of the 7th millennium BP. Soon the population was dispersed in hamlets and villages over the available area. Larger settlements provided additional services that the hamlets themselves could not.

SUMER

Sumer, located in the southernmost part of Mesopotamia, between the Tigris and Euphrates rivers, was the home of one of the first civilizations, Sumeria. Sumeria's Early Dynastic Phase began about 5000 BP, a century or so after the development of a nuanced writing system based on the Sumerian language. Barley was the main crop, but wheat, flax (*Linum* species), dates (*Phoenix* species), apples (*Malus* species), plums (*Prunus* species), and grapes (*Vitaceae* species) were also grown. This was the period during which the earliest known evidence of carefully bred sheep and goats has been found; these animals were more numerous than cattle and were kept mainly for meat, milk, butter,

Onager (Equus hemionus onager) *mare and foal.* Kenneth W. Fink/Bruce Coleman Inc.

and cheese. It has been estimated that at Ur, a large town covering some 50 acres (20 hectares) within a cultivated enclave, there were 10,000 animals confined in sheepfolds and stables, of which 3,000 were slaughtered each year. Ur's population of about 6,000 people included a labour force of 2,500 who annually cultivated 3,000 acres of land (some 1,200 hectares), leaving an equal amount of land fallow. The workforce included storehouse recorders, work foremen, overseers, and harvest supervisors, as well as labourers. Agricultural produce was allocated to temple personnel in return for their services, to important people in the community, and to small farmers.

The land was cultivated by teams of oxen pulling light unwheeled plows, and the grain was harvested with sickles in the spring. Wagons had solid wheels with leather tires held in position by copper nails. They were drawn by oxen or onagers (wild asses) that were harnessed by collars, yokes, and headstalls and controlled by reins and a ring through the nose or upper lip and a strap under the jaw. As many as four animals, harnessed abreast to a central pole, pulled a wagon. The horse, which was probably domesticated about 6000 BP by pastoral nomads in what is now Ukraine, did not displace the heartier onager as a draft animal in the region until about 4000 BP. Soon after, written instructions appeared for the grooming, exercising, and medication of horses; presumably for breeding purposes, horses were named and records of sires kept. During the summer months, the upper highland areas were exploited by nomads who inhabited the lower-lying regions during the cooler seasons.

THE NILE VALLEY

In ancient Egypt, agricultural exploitation apparently did not intensify until domesticated animals from Southwest Asia were introduced. By the first quarter of the 7th millennium BP in Al-Fayyūm, some villages were keeping sheep, goats, and swine and cultivating emmer, barley, cotton, and flax, which was woven into linen. In this dry climate, village silos consisted of pits lined with coiled basketry; crops were harvested with reaping knives slotted with sharp flints. Elsewhere, at Al-Badarī in Upper Egypt, animals were also kept. The fact that dead domesticated animals were wrapped in linen and then buried close to villages may indicate that agriculture was closely associated with some form of religious belief.

By the time of the predynastic Amratian culture, about 5550 BP, agriculture appears to have begun in the valley alluviums of the Nile. By late predynastic times, about 5050 BP, there is evidence of a considerable growth in wealth deriving from agricultural development and accompanied by a more hierarchical social system.

Depictions on tombs and artifacts from the dynastic periods indicate that, in addition to present-day domesticates, animals such as the gazelle, deer (*Cervidae* species),

A relief from Egypt's 4th Dynasty depicting a wheat harvest.
DEA/A. Dagli Orti/De Agostini/Getty Images

hyena (*Hyaenidae* species), and aoudad, or Barbary sheep (*Ammotragus lervia*), were kept either in captivity or under some form of control. Whether this can be regarded as domestication is unclear, but certainly some aspects of animal husbandry were practiced with these unusual animals. Some early villages in Egypt relied heavily on gazelles as a food source. According to some scholars, incipient gazelle domestication may have been under way during the predynastic period, but other researchers have challenged this hypothesis. It has also been suggested that millet was a staple crop in ancient Egypt.

By the beginning of Egypt's 4th dynasty, about 4525 BP, agriculture had become a sophisticated enterprise. In contrast to Mesopotamia, where the tendency had been to develop urbanized communities, Egypt had cities that tended to be no more than market towns to serve the surrounding countryside. A whole bureaucracy dealt with agriculture. The grand vizier, second only to the pharaoh, stood at its head, and the ministry of agriculture stood under him. There was a chief of the fields and a master of largesse, who looked after the livestock. There were royal domains and temple estates. Between landlord and tenant there was a patriarchal relationship, which, although despotic, was underlain by a strong sense of responsibility to the land. Rent was three and a half bushels of grain to the acre.

Irrigation and the waters of the Nile were carefully controlled. Records show that King Menes, who lived about 4875 BP, had a large masonry dam built to control the Nile River and provide water for irrigation. A millennium later the Nile at flood was diverted through a channel 12 miles (19 km) long into Lake Moeris so that, after the flood, water in the lake could be released for irrigation. Seed grain was lent to tenants, and teams of oxen were lent or hired to them. The land was tilled with a wooden plow

NILE RIVER IRRIGATION

As an aid to cultivation, irrigation almost certainly originated in Egypt. A particular phenomenon that makes irrigation from the Nile feasible is the slope of the land from south to north—which amounts to about 5 inches (13 cm) to the mile (1.6 km)—as well as the slightly greater slope downward from the riverbanks to the desert on either side.

The first use of the Nile for irrigation in Egypt began when seeds were sown in the mud left after the annual floodwater had subsided. With the passing of time, these practices were refined until a traditional method emerged, known as basin irrigation.

A stand of sugarcane on the west bank of the Nile River, near Dandarah, Egypt. Bob Burch/Bruce Coleman Inc.

Under this system, the fields on the flat floodplain were divided by earth banks into a series of large basins of varying size but some as large as 50,000 acres (20,000 hectares). During the annual Nile flood, the basins were flooded and the water allowed to remain on the fields for up to six weeks. The water was then permitted to drain away as the river level fell, and a thin deposit of rich Nile silt was left on the land each year. Autumn and winter crops were then sown in the waterlogged soil. Under this system only one crop per year could be grown on the land, and the farmer was always at the mercy of annual fluctuations in the size of the flood.

drawn by an ox or an ass. The land was plowed twice, once to break the ground, after which the clods were broken up by heavy hoes, and a second time to cover the seed. Six-rowed barley and emmer wheat were the main crops. The seed was sown by a funnel on the plow or, alternatively, was trodden in by sheep. The crops were cut with sickles, which had been improved by the introduction of a curved blade. The harvest produced 11 times the sowing, but it is not known whether or not two crops were grown within the year. The grain was threshed by asses or cattle treading on it on the threshing floor. It was winnowed by tossing in the wind, which caused the chaff to blow away and the grain to fall back into the basket, and was then stored in great silos. Lentils, beans, flax, and onions (*Allium* species) were other important Egyptian field crops.

The production of animals for food was also important, and records indicate that people raised cattle (black, piebald, and white), sheep with kempy (coarse) coats, goats, pigs, and domesticated ducks and geese. One wealthy landlord in the 6th dynasty owned 1,000 cattle, 760 asses, 2,200 goats, and 1,000 sheep. Animal breeding for specialized purposes was also developed: one breed of cattle was kept for meat and another for milk; a Saluki-like hunting dog was bred; and a type of fat-tailed sheep was developed for meat and milk.

MESOAMERICA

An understanding of Mesoamerican agricultural origins is hampered by the fact that few archaeological sites pertinent to the question have been explored. The Guilá Naquitz site in southern Mexico has some of the earliest evidence for the shift to food production in Mesoamerica, including extensive evidence for the use of acorn (*Quercus* species), piñon pine nut (*Pinus edulis*), prickly pear (*Opuntia* species), mesquite seeds (*Prosopis* species), wild runner bean, and the seeds of various grasses. Several squash seeds that are larger than those from wild squashes have also been found at this site, indicating that domestication was occurring. One of the largest of these seeds has been directly dated to 10,000 BP, making it among the oldest evidence for a domesticated plant in the Americas. Local experimentation with foxtail grass seems to have led to a failed domestication attempt. Pollen from domesticated corn and manioc has been found in levels dating to 7000–6000 BP at the San Andrés site in the gulf coast of Tabasco, Mex. Cotton pollen and seeds that may be from the domesticated sunflower (*Helianthus* species) have also been recovered there and dated to 4600 BP. However, the sunflower is problematic because all available evidence is for its domestication in eastern North America, suggesting that the Mexican specimens may belong to another species. Low-density, highly mobile Preceramic populations were responsible for these developments.

Despite the prominence of corn in the late archaeological record of Mesoamerica, the origins of this crop are still not clearly understood. The oldest recovered corn cob is from Guilá Naquitz and dates to between 6300 and 6000 BP, but corn was probably not domesticated in this part of Mexico, because it appears suddenly and in an already domesticated form. Among the wild grasses—including teosintes (e.g., *Zea diploperennis* and *Z. mays parviglumis*), the best candidates for the wild ancestor of corn—none have the extraordinarily robust and productive cob structure of corn. In one model a series of massive mutations has been proposed to account for the development of the corn cob, but how to account for these mutations is problematic. Instead of requiring mutations, a recent genetic analysis indicates that a third grass, gamma grass (*Tripsacum dactyloides*), crossed with teosinte to produce a hybrid with the cob structure typical of corn. Although teosinte is not particularly palatable, *Tripsacum* has a history of being used for food. People may have recognized teosinte-*Tripsacum* crosses in the wild and selected them for planting. Another possibility is that teosinte and early corn were exploited first for the sugar content of their stalks and leaves. Ancient Mexicans chewed the leaves and stalks of early corn for their sweet flavour, and the sugar and starch from corn were also useful in making alcohol, an important comestible in many types of social interactions. Corn kernels would have been less important in these contexts, making it less likely that they would be preserved. This might help explain the rarity of corn in the early archaeological record. Whatever its origins, corn became a staple crop of the Americas, where it was often prepared as a potage or by boiling in limewater and grinding. Cornmeal paste was then made into tortillas, flat cakes, or gruel.

Villages did not become common in the Americas until the so-called Early Formative period, which began about 3800 BP, after corn was domesticated. Village life was based on the extended family, composed of parents and their children's families, who formed the labour force. Villages were organized into larger territorial units based on ceremonial centres that commonly featured flat-topped pyramids. Eventually, Formative groups such as the Olmec, known for carving colossal stone heads, developed large prosperous towns. Larger territorial units developed about 2000 BP, and Formative cultures were eventually eclipsed by the Maya, Toltec, and Aztec empires. Food was supplied to these empires' large urban centres by a combination of rain-fed swidden fields and gardens and irrigated tropical lowland field systems.

Prominent crops in Mesoamerica eventually included avocados, cacao, chili peppers, cotton, common beans, lima beans, corn, manioc, tomatoes, and quinoa (*Chenopodium quinoa* subspecies). The principal domestic animals were the turkey, dog, and Muscovy duck. Irrigation, terracing, and the use of artificial islands (*chinampas*) increased land usage in areas with less precipitation. The land was cleared by chopping and burning, and the seeds were sown with the aid of fire-hardened digging sticks. Crops were stored in pits or granaries. It is apparent that much remains to be learned about early agriculture in the Mesoamerican lowlands.

SOUTH AMERICA

In the highlands of south-central Chile, potatoes were collected as early as 14,000 BP. By 5000 BP the domesticated potato is found in desert coastal sites; it was apparently domesticated well before that time. Between 14,000 and 8000 BP the *cavi*, or guinea pig, was economically important; it was probably domesticated by 3000 BP. Wild camelids were hunted as early as 10,000 BP; by 7500–6000 BP llama and alpaca remains are so common in archaeological sites that they had probably been domesticated as well. Quinoa was harvested by 7500 BP and cotton by 6000 BP in northern Peru.

Highland sites have also yielded squash (c. 10,400– 10,000 BP) and peanuts (c. 8500 BP). However, these cultigens were introduced to the Andes in fully domesticated form, indicating they were important in the lowlands at the same time or earlier. Thus, the development of successful tropical lowland swidden systems with crops such as avocados, cacao, chili peppers, cotton, manioc, corn, papayas, sweet potatoes, and tobacco may have a long history in the Amazon basin. Lowland sites have yielded the phytoliths (microscopic particles that are formed by plants and are resistant to decomposition) of domesticated plants such as bottle gourd (*Lageneria siceraria*), squash, and corn that date to between 8000 and 7000 BP. However, this evidence is controversial because phytoliths cannot yet be directly dated.

The 8000–7000 BP phytolith date for early corn has also been questioned because it challenges the timing of the domestication of corn in Mexico, which seems to be the more likely site for this transformation. Corn remains directly dated to 3500 BP have been recovered from coastal Ecuador and are reported from the interior a few centuries later. These remains are consistent with an earlier domestication in Mexico followed by a southward dispersal to South America. Additional directly dated corn remains will be necessary to sort out the complex issue of this plant's initial domestication and spread.

The lima bean and the common bean are two other significant crops that became widespread in the Americas. Both appear to have been domesticated in the southern Andes. The oldest domesticated lima beans come from the Peruvian desert coast and date to between 7000 and 5000 BP; however, as this plant was domesticated in the highlands, it must have become a cultigen well before 7000 BP. The oldest common bean in the Americas is from Guitarrero Cave (Peru) and is directly dated to 4300 BP. Lima beans at the same site date to 3400 BP.

Studies of pollen and charcoal retrieved from ancient sediments around Lake Ayauch (Ecuador), in the western Amazon, indicate that the earliest forest clearance and burning normally associated with swidden agriculture occurred there about 5000 BP or slightly earlier. Between 4500 and 2000 BP these activities had also intensified in the eastern Amazon. Tropical lowland slash-and-burn agriculture was apparently practiced throughout the Amazon basin by that time. Ceramic griddles used to cook bitter manioc appear about 4000 BP. The long history of swidden production is related to its appropriateness for the tropical lowlands: it helped to maintain local soil fertility and mimicked the ecologically diverse tropical ecosystem. Further, labour-intensive technology was not required. Some researchers have proposed that the nature of tropical lowland ecosystems cannot be understood without acknowledging the long-term presence of swidden agriculture.

Agriculture eventually came to support the Inca empire and other highland South American cultures. The problems of maintaining large populations in the highlands were resolved through an agricultural system supported by terracing, irrigation, and fertilizers.

NORTH AMERICA

The regions north of the Rio Grande saw the origin of three, or perhaps four, agricultural complexes. Two of these developed in what is now the southwestern United States. The Upper Sonoran complex included corn, squash, bottle gourd, and the common bean and was found where rainfall was greater than about 8 inches (200 mm) annually. The Lower Sonoran complex, with less annual precipitation, included corn, squash, cotton, and beans—tepary bean, lima bean, scarlet runner bean, and jack bean (*Canavalia ensiformis*).

Corn appears to have been the first cultigen in the Southwest. Direct radiocarbon dates place it at the Bat Cave site in the Mogollon highlands of New Mexico by 3200 BP, where squash is also present. The first beans appear about 1500 BP. These crops were integrated into the diets of Archaic cultures—groups characterized by high mobility, no pottery, and extensive plant use, including grain harvesting. The Southwestern Archaic system may have been similar to those of the traditional Paiute and Kumeyaay (one branch of the Diegueño Indians), who did not practice agriculture per se but who had developed an agroecosystem. In agroecosystems, people actively planted flora in order to increase the diversity of available plant resources. They also harvested wild grass seeds, separating the grain heads from the stalks by pulling or cutting. The stalks were gathered into sheaves. After harvesting, they burned the grass and then broadcast some of the seeds over the burned area, consuming the rest. Economically important plants were concentrated around their settlements as a result of these actions.

In most of the Southwest, the Archaic lifestyle was transformed to a more sedentary system supported by food production soon after 1700 BP. By 900 BP, Ancestral Pueblo (Anasazi), Hohokam, and Mogollon communities had become widespread. These groups used a variety of agricultural techniques: crops were grown on alluvium caught behind check dams, low walls built in arroyos to catch runoff from the limited rains; hillside contour terraces helped conserve soil and water; and bordered gardens and irrigation systems were devised. At Snaketown, a Hohokam site in Arizona, a complex canal system supported a large urban population. Many canals were at least 6.5 feet (2 metres) deep and 10 feet (3 metres) wide. In the nearby Phoenix area, hundreds of miles of canals have been found.

The third agricultural regime in North America was found in the eastern part of the continent. It originated in the region between the Mississippi River and the Appalachian Mountains, an area that includes the rich watersheds of rivers such as the Illinois, Kentucky, and Tennessee. Plants of the Eastern Agricultural Complex included sunflower, squash, a native chenopod (*Chenopodium berlandieri*), amaranth (*Amaranthus* species), maygrass (*Phalaris caroliniana*), sumpweed (*Iva annua*), little barley (*Hordeum pusillum*), and possibly erect knotweed (*Polygonum erectum*). Fish, shellfish, deer, acorns, walnuts (*Juglans* species), and hickory nuts (*Carya* species) were also important.

An agroecology similar to that proposed for the Archaic Southwest probably existed among the Eastern Archaic peoples, but it has been difficult to document. Eastern groups had well-established bases from which they foraged, including shell mound sites used for thousands of years in Kentucky and Tennessee. At the Koster site in Illinois, a semipermanent village dates to 8400 BP, and a more permanent settlement was occupied beginning about 5900 BP.

The earliest locally domesticated plant in the region is squash; examples appear between 8000 and 5000 BP on sites in Missouri, Illinois, Kentucky, Pennsylvania, and Maine. Squash seeds from the Phillips Spring site (Missouri) date to about 5000 BP and are within the size range of domesticated squash. Although a squash was domesticated in Mesoamerica by 10,000 BP, genetic and biochemical research indicates that the squashes in eastern North America are a separate subspecies that was domesticated locally.

Another early local cultigen is sumpweed. A drastic change in seed size indicates that wild sumpweed fruits were harvested in Illinois about 7000 BP and that by 5500 BP a domesticated, large-seeded sumpweed was being grown. The average size of sumpweed seeds continued to enlarge until about 500 BP, when the domesticated form became extinct, but wild forms have persisted.

Sunflower is another crop that was domesticated in the East. Small wild sunflower fruits are reported from the Koster site in an occupation dating to about 9000 BP. By 5000 BP at the Hayes site in Tennessee, larger domesticated sunflower fruits are reported. Wild sunflower is not native to the East. Rather, wild sunflower appears to have been introduced somehow from the Colorado Plateau in the U.S. Southwest. Sunflower was never domesticated there, however; sometime after the start of the European conquest, domesticated sunflower was introduced to the region from the East.

Chenopod domestication in the East dates to at least 4500 BP, when thin-seed-coat specimens appear at the Cloudsplitter and Newt Kash rock shelters in Kentucky. Extensive collection of chenopod fruits began even earlier in Illinois.

Eastern Archaic peoples were becoming increasingly sedentary by about 4000–3000 BP. At Poverty Point in the lower Mississippi valley (now Poverty Point National Monument), people built a complex set of geometrically arranged mounds that date to between 3800 and 3400 BP. By 3000 BP the Eastern Agricultural Complex supported a complex socioeconomic system exemplified by cultures such as the Adena and its descendant, the Hopewell. In much of the region, communities became fully sedentary.

A sunflower seed dating to about 3500 BP, found at an excavation site in Kentucky. John Steiner, Smithsonian Institution

In addition, pottery had become common, mound complexes began to be built over a wide area, and populations were growing rapidly.

Also at about 3000 BP, archaeological sites on the Cumberland Plateau of Kentucky provide clear evidence that fire was being used to clear garden plots. Burning was widely used in aboriginal North America as a technique for clearing the forest understory; it was also used to maintain stands of fire-tolerant species such as oak. By creating forest openings and edges that exposed the trees to more sunlight and less competition, burning encouraged more nut production.

The earliest corn in the East appears in the central Mississippi valley about 2100 BP. The introduction of corn did not displace the use of locally domesticated plants. Instead, it seems to have been an addition that did not immediately have an obvious impact. By 1600 BP corn was grown as far north as Ontario, Can., where no form of crop production had previously existed. By 1500 BP the Hopewell pattern ceased. Two distinct systems followed, the Mississippian and the Late Woodland, both eventually supported by corn agriculture. In the Mississippi valley and the Southeast, urban centres with temple mound architecture had developed by 1000 BP. At almost the same time in the Northeast, people were beginning to establish longhouse villages and towns. The common bean was not incorporated into agricultural production until about 800 years ago. By then substantial socioeconomic changes resulting from agriculture had transformed the human landscape across the region.

The region from southern British Columbia through California and west to the Great Basin is increasingly being considered as the domain of a fourth agricultural regime. Nearly all of the native peoples living in this region managed habitats and plants, and some had small gardens at the time of European contact. Perhaps because the first Europeans to visit the region did not witness the extensive geometric field production of grains with which they were familiar, they assumed the indigenous peoples did not have agriculture. Nevertheless, people such as the Owens Valley Paiute irrigated the grasses they used for subsistence. Other groups used controlled burning to manage oak stands and increase acorn production, often planting tobacco in the burned areas. Another management technique was to tend sedges (*Cyperaceae* family) so that the rhizomes became long and unbranched, a practice that made the plants easier to harvest. These complex plant and habitat management practices blur the distinctions between hunter-gatherers and farmers to the extent that many anthropologists are no longer classifying these people as hunter-gatherers per se.

CHAPTER 3

EARLY AGRICULTURE IN ASIA

On his way across the Pamirs in search of Buddhist texts (518 CE), the Chinese pilgrim Song Yun noted that the crest of the bare, cold, snowy highlands was commonly believed to be "the middle point of heaven and earth":

> *The people of this region use the water of the rivers for irrigating their lands; and when they were told that in the middle country* [China] *the fields were watered by the rain, they laughed and said, "How could heaven provide enough for all?"*

Yet, heaven provided. The vast majority of the population of Asia lives in the regions between the inland mountains and the seas—from Pakistan through India, Myanmar (Burma), Thailand, Laos, Cambodia, Vietnam, and eastern China up to the Bo Hai (Gulf of Chihli) and the offshore island groups of Japan, Malaysia, Indonesia, the Philippines, and Sri Lanka. In the early 21st century some 2.5 billion people were concentrated in just two of these countries, China and India.

There is no consensus on the origin and progress of plant and animal domestication in Asia. The Soviet plant geneticist Nikolay Ivanovich Vavilov postulated several world centres of plant origin, of which

Herding goats along the ancient Silk Road, northern Takla Makan Desert, China. Bob Thomason/Tony Stone Worldwide

an unusual wealth of original genera, species, and varieties of plants is found in India and China, countries which have contributed almost half of our crop plants.

CHINA

From earliest times, agriculture in China has been divided into two major regions by the Qin Mountains, with wheat and millet predominant in the northern realm and rice in the south. At different periods and places, subsidiary native domesticates have included soybeans; tree fruits such as peach and persimmon; hemp (*Cannabis sativa*); beefsteak plant (*Perilla frutescens*); rapeseed, or canola (*Brassica campestris*); tea (*Camellia sinensis*); water chestnut (*Trapa natans*); and silk (via sericulture, the raising of silkworms). Domesticated animals have included dogs, pigs, chickens, goats, and cattle.

EARLY HISTORY

Although few archaeological data have been recovered from the period from roughly 12,000 to 9000 BP in China, the presence of settlements in Japan at that time suggests that further investigations will reveal analogous developments on the continent. Settled communities are first evident between 9000 and 8000 BP in Inner Mongolia and the Huangtu Gaoyuan (Loess Plateau) drained by the Huang He (Yellow River) system and other rivers such as the Liao in northeastern China. In all these areas, people were moving toward agriculture by 8000 BP.

Although the northern regions are relatively dry today, they were wetter in the past; river valley locations would have further ameliorated regional aridity. Early settlements consisted of groups of pit houses, a form of architecture that provides natural insulation and, given the labour involved in construction, represents a long-term commitment to a particular locale. The Xinglongwa culture in Inner Mongolia began sometime just before 8000 BP and had well-developed stone and pottery technology, broomcorn millet, rectangular houses arranged in rows with a ditch surrounding the community, and burials of people and pigs below some house floors. The immediate predecessor of this culture is not yet known. At Peiligang (north-central Henan) and Cishan (southern Hebei), numerous oval and rectangular houses are associated with large storage pits. Excavations at Yuchanyan Cave (Hunan) in the early 21st century yielded pottery that was dated 18,300 to 15,430 BP. It was discovered in what was believed to be a Late Paleolithic foragers' camp and is the oldest pottery discovered to date.

Crops domesticated in the north include foxtail and broomcorn millet, both well adapted to dry climates with short growing seasons. The ancestor of foxtail millet is green foxtail grass (*Seteria italica viridis*), while the ancestor of broomcorn millet has yet to be identified. Domesticated millet grains are distinguished from wild

Ceramic funerary urn from Yangshao, Henan province, c. 3000 BCE; in the Museum of Far Eastern Antiquities, Stockholm. Ostasiatiska Museet, Stockholm

grains by changes in their proportions and size. Both foxtail and broomcorn millet seeds are somewhat spherical, while their wild counterparts are flat and thin. Each domesticated grain has considerably more food value than the wild grain. Hemp also became an important fibre and oil crop, although the archaeological record for the plant is poor. Members of the mustard family, such as Chinese cabbage, were also being domesticated. Some of the earliest domesticated chickens are found here, as are swine. Notably, the East Asian pig was domesticated independently from that domesticated in western Asia and Europe.

As elsewhere, early domesticates were successful additions to an economic system that still included significant input from wild resources. The addition of these resources permitted communities to grow more numerous and populous by 6000 BP. During this period, regional pottery styles were well developed; the distribution of such styles indicates clear zones of habitual interaction over long distances. For instance, people with a sophisticated painted pottery complex known as the Yangshao dominated the Huang He catchment region. The Yangshao culture is notable for its kiln-fired pottery, which has black symbols and animals painted on a yellowish-orange background. Yangshao sites such as Banpocun (Shaanxi) were occupied for centuries; pit houses, storage pits, kilns, a cemetery, animal pens, and mortars and pestles for grinding grain have all been identified there. Much of Banpocun is surrounded by a moat a number of feet deep.

Early agricultural communities in southern China were located close to water, because rice could be grown only in seasonally inundated habitats such as lake and marsh margins; paddy fields may have been in use, but rice grown without paddy fields could still be found in China in historical times. In this subtropical monsoonal region, the complex lake systems along the Yangtze basin in south-central China acted as catch basins for floodwaters and wetlands and provided an ideal setting for early rice exploitation.

In this region, rice appears to have been exploited long before the first evidence for its domestication. Rock shelter or cave sites such as Diaotonghuan and Xianrendong, near Dongting Lake, have deposits older than 10,000 BP with evidence of wild rice use. Wild rice was likely growing in the nearby marshy lowlands, now filled in. Rice phytoliths, mainly from chaff, have been found in soils from Diaotunghuan, a rock shelter approximately 200 feet (60 metres) above the wet Dayuan basin, making it highly unlikely the phytoliths came into the shelter naturally. The site's earliest rice phytoliths date well before 10,000 BP and are all from wild rice. By 8000 BP the phytoliths resemble those from domesticated rice.

Archaeological sites that are waterlogged but otherwise stable tend to have excellent organic preservation; such is the case at the Yangtze floodplain village of Bashidang, where a 1,075-square-foot (100-square-metre) area of wet deposits has yielded some 15,000 rice grains. Domesticated rice remains directly dated to 8500 BP are found at Bashidang and at another site, Pengtoushan. These sites belong to what Chinese archaeologists call the Pengtoushan culture, whose radiocarbon dates cluster from 9500 to 8100 BP. The sites each cover about 7.5 acres (3 hectares). Bashidang has some of the earliest defensive walls and ditches found in China.

Much earlier claims for rice domestication have been made, but the evidence is currently weak. One outstanding issue in rice domestication is the origin of the plant's two prominent subspecies, *Oryza sativa japonica* and *O. sativa indica*. Interestingly, the Bashidang rice evinces considerable variation and belongs to neither subspecies.

Another site dating to about the same period is Kuahuqiao, located near Hangzhou Bay. The economy at Kuahuqiao was not strictly dependent on agriculture, emphasizing instead a balance of food production, hunting, gathering, and fishing. The site was occupied for only a few centuries, then abandoned because of rising sea levels. Evidence indicates that people regularly burned the area near the site, possibly to clear the land for rice production. Rice was grown there, but other foods such as acorns seem to have been more important. People also ate peaches and plums as well as prickly water lily (*Euryale ferox*), water chestnut (*Trapa* species), and lotus root (*Nelumbo nucifera*). The dog is common at the site, and people fished and hunted a wide range of waterfowl and deer.

The best example of an early community substantially dependent on rice production is Hemudu (6500–5500 BP), a site located on the south side of Hangzhou Bay, not far from Shanghai. Constructed in a wet area, wood-frame houses there were built on pilings to keep floors dry. Dogs, pigs, water buffalo, bottle gourds, water caltrop, and rice were all present.

By 4500 BP the Longshan culture, generally viewed as ancestral to state societies in North China, stretched from the Huang He to the Shandong Peninsula. In some areas, Longshan people had added rice to their repertoire of crops.

THE CLASSICAL-IMPERIAL ERA

About 335 BCE China's potential cropland was so expansive that the philosopher Mencius wrote, "If the farmer's seasons are not interfered with, there will be more grain in the land than can be consumed." By the 1st century BCE, however, wastelands were being reclaimed for cultivation, and there was a demand for limitation of landholdings. About 9 CE the first (unsuccessful) attempt was made to "nationalize" the land and distribute it among the peasants. By the end of the 2nd century CE, severe agrarian crises culminating generally in the downfall of the ruling dynasty had become a recurrent theme of history. Through the centuries, then, much of Chinese agriculture has been characterized by a struggle to raise ever more food.

By the 4th century CE, cultivation was more intensive in China than in Europe or the rest of Asia. The major cereal-producing region and the population, however, were shifting rapidly from the wheat and millet area of the North China Plain to the paddies of the lower Yangtze valley. By the 8th century the lower Yangtze was exporting enormous quantities of grain into the old northwest by way of a unified system of canals linking the large rivers.

By about 1100 CE the population of South China had probably tripled, while that of the whole country may have exceeded 100 million. Consequently, cultivation became extremely intensive, with a family of 10 living, for example, on a farm of about 14 acres (5.6 hectares). Again, more new lands were opened to cultivation. Even tanks, ponds, reservoirs, streams, and creeks were reclaimed to be turned into farms. At the same time, complex water-driven machinery came into use for pumping irrigation water onto fields, for draining them, and for threshing and milling grain. A large variety of improved and complicated field implements were also employed; these are described and illustrated in the agricultural literature of the day.

TOOLS AND TECHNIQUES

The first significant revolution in Chinese agricultural technology occurred when iron agricultural implements became available to the Chinese peasantry. The earliest iron plow found in northern Henan dates from the Warring States period (475–221 BCE) and is a flat V-shaped iron piece that must have been mounted on wooden blades and handles. It was small, and there is no evidence that draft animals were used. Cattle-drawn plows do not appear until the 1st century BCE.

Several improvements and innovations, such as the three-shared plow, the *louli* (plow-and-sow) implement, and the harrow, were developed subsequently. By the end of the Song dynasty in 1279, Chinese agricultural engineering had reached a high state of development.

The common farmers continued to use these early medieval techniques into modern times. Their unfenced fields were cultivated by a wooden plow, with or without a cast-iron share and usually drawn by a water buffalo. Harvesting was by sickle or billhook (a cutting tool consisting of a blade with a hooked point fitted with a handle). Sheaves carried from the field were slung at the ends of a pole across an individual's shoulders. The grain was threshed by beating on a frame of slats or by flails on the ground. Winnowing was accomplished by tossing the grain in the wind. Rice was husked by hand pounding in a mortar or with a hand-turned mill. Irrigation techniques varied. The most common perhaps was a wooden, square-paddle chain pump with a radial treadle operated by foot. Fields were drained by open ditches and diking. Human feces, oil cakes, and ash fertilized the soil.

Over the past millennium, the revolution in Chinese agriculture was not in mechanical or chemical technology but rather in the biological sphere: in crops, cropping systems, and land utilization. Under increasing population pressures, cultivation was forced to become more labour-intensive and also to expand into the sandy loams, the arid hills, and the upper reaches of lofty mountains. Lacking major technological inventions, the Chinese peasant had to expand the area under cultivation by finding suitable crops for inferior land.

LAND USE

A "three fields in two years" rotation system for wheat and millet was being practiced by the 6th century CE. Revolutionary changes in land utilization, however, started with the introduction in Fujian province of an early-maturing and relatively drought-resistant rice from Champa, a kingdom in what is now Vietnam. In 1012, when there was a drought in the lower Yangtze and Huai River regions, 30,000 bushels of Champa seeds were distributed. Usually a summer crop, the native rice plant of these locales required 150 days to mature after transplanting. Not only did this make a second crop difficult, but, because of the plant's soil and water requirements, cultivation was confined largely to the deltas, basins, and valleys of the Yangtze. The imported Champa rice, on the other hand, ripened in just 100 days after transplanting and required less water.

The success of Champa rice initiated the development and dissemination of many more varieties suited to local peculiarities of soil, temperature, and crop rotation. The first new early-ripening strain to develop required 60 days after transplantation. By the 18th century a 50-day Champa and a 40-day Champa had been developed. In 1834 a 30-day variety was available—probably the quickest-ripening rice ever recorded. The effect was revolutionary. By the 13th century, much of the hilly land of the lower Yangtze region and Fujian had been turned into terraced paddies. At the close of the 16th century, Champa rice had made double, and sometimes triple, crops of rice common.

A second revolution in land utilization began in the 16th century, with the adoption of food crops from the Americas, such as corn, sweet potatoes, potatoes, and peanuts (groundnuts). These could be grown at drier altitudes and in sandy loams too light for rice and other indigenous cereals. Virgin heights in the Yangtze region and northern China were turned into corn and sweet-potato farms. As the population in the mountain districts increased, the potato took over the soils too poor for those crops. By the middle of the 19th century, even ravines and remote mountains were being cultivated. Similarly, the cultivation of peanuts penetrated the remote and agriculturally backward areas of Guangdong, Guangxi, and Yunnan provinces and the sandbars of Sichuan. Gradually, they brought about a revolution in the utilization of sandy soils along the lower Yangtze, the lower Huang He, the southeast coast, particularly Fujian and Guangdong, and numerous inland rivers and streams.

Even so, the revolution in land use failed to alter the basic human-land relationship in China. In the 18th century the Qianlong emperor rejected renewed demands for limitation of land ownership. In an edict (1740), however, he noted that "the population is constantly increasing, while the land does not become any more extensive." He directed his subjects, therefore, to cultivate all and every odd piece of soil,

> *on top of the mountains or at the corners of the land. All these soils are suitable either for rice or for miscellaneous crops....No matter how little return the people may receive from cultivation of these lands, it will be always helpful in supplying food provisions for the people.*

RICE

The edible starchy cereal grain known as rice is among the most important crops for human subsistence. Roughly one-half of the world's population, including virtually all of East and Southeast Asia, is wholly dependent upon rice as a staple food. Some 95 percent of the world's rice crop is eaten by humans.

The cultivated rice plant, *Oryza sativa*, is an annual grass of the Gramineae family. It grows to about 4 feet (1.2 metres) in height. The leaves are long and flattened, and its panicle, or inflorescence, is made up of spikelets bearing flowers that produce the fruit, or grain.

Many cultures have evidence of early rice cultivation, including China, India, and the civilizations of Southeast Asia. However, the earliest archaeological evidence comes from central and eastern China and dates to 7000–5000 BC. With the exception of the type called upland rice, the plant is grown on submerged land in the coastal plains, tidal deltas, and river basins of tropical, semitropical, and temperate regions. The seeds are sown in prepared beds, and when the seedlings are 25 to 50 days old, they are transplanted to a field, or paddy, that has been enclosed by levees and submerged under 2 to 4 inches (5 to 10 cm) of water, remaining submerged during the growing season.

KOREA

Between at least 8000 and 4000 BP the Chulmun culture flourished in the Korean peninsula. Chulmun people lived in pit-house villages and made pottery that was undecorated or decorated with linear designs. Their economy seems to have been based largely on hunting, gathering, and fishing. Foxtail millet and broomcorn millet directly dated to 5500 BP were discovered at the Tongsamdong site, near Pusan in southern South Korea. By 4000 BP rice appears to have been introduced from China.

Despite the initial adoption of crop production by Chulmun peoples, intensive agriculture did not develop in Korea until the beginning of the Bronze Age Mumun period, between 3500 and 3000 BP, when significant socio-economic changes spread throughout the peninsula. Rice was more extensively grown during the Mumun period, and bread wheat (*Triticum aestivum*), soybean, adzuki (red) bean, and hemp were also grown. The original sources for soybeans and adzuki beans are still unclear, although early Chinese records mention that soybeans were a gift from the region encompassing the Northeast Plain (formerly Manchuria) and Korea. Korean soybeans dating to about 3000 BP are the oldest yet discovered. Mumun ridged dry fields and paddy fields have been excavated in the southern Korean peninsula.

JAPAN

In Japan, archaeologists have established a long unbroken sequence of cultures that spans the period from more than 30,000 years ago to the present. Villages were established throughout the Japanese archipelago between 13,000 and 11,000 BP. The oldest pottery in the world is found in Japan, China, and eastern Siberia and is associated with radiocarbon dates of about 13,800–13,000 BP. Extensive settlements in East Asia appear first in Japan at the beginning of the Jōmon period; the Uenohara site, in Kyushu, an Initial Jōmon pit-house community, dates to 11,000–8000 BP.

The early Jōmon were managing various plant resources and so are probably best described as food producers rather than strictly hunters and gatherers. Lacquer production was under way in northern Japan by 9000 BP, suggesting the so-called varnish tree (*Rhus verniciflua*) was being managed. At sites such as Usujiri B and Hamanasuno, in southwestern Hokkaido, small wild grains were harvested, as were fleshy fruits and nuts; as a result of human activity, the productivity of fruit- and nut-bearing trees was especially high near Jōmon communities.

By 4000 BP seeds of wild barnyard grass increased in size and became indistinguishable from those of its domesticated descendant, barnyard millet, in southwestern Hokkaido sites; this indicates that the Jōmon domesticated at least one plant. By about the same time, they had developed an elaborate culture characterized by ornate pottery, an extensive stone tool kit, and probably social ranking. Population densities were within the range of what might be expected for agriculturalists, suggesting that these Japanese peoples were living lives similar to those led by early Chinese agriculturists a few millennia before. Chinese crops such as hemp, foxtail and broomcorn millets, and rice were in Japan by 3,000 years ago; at about the same time, earthworks associated with cemeteries began to become common in the north.

By 3000–2500 BP, social and technological changes seen at least 500 years earlier in Korea were reaching the southern Japanese archipelago. These included paddy agriculture, bronze, and iron; the transformation produced the Yayoi culture. The Yayoi are known for metallurgy, intensive agriculture, and more-centralized sociopolitical organization. The Itazuke site has evidence of well-engineered drainage systems that were used to maintain paddy fields, and ditches and earthworks served as defensive structures around this and other densely populated communities. Crops included rice, millet, wheat, barley, soybeans, adzuki beans, hops, bottle gourds, peaches, and persimmons.

The Yayoi transformation expanded toward the northeast, and by 2100 BP all but Hokkaido, the northernmost prefecture, was part of the Yayoi world. In the south the Yayoi culture moved mainly through migration, but in the north Jōmon people appear to have adopted aspects of Yayoi life, including intensive agriculture. Yayoi crops were not entirely new to northeastern Japan; the region's oldest directly dated rice, foxtail millet, and broomcorn millet are from Late Jōmon contexts (2900 BP) at the Kazahari site in Aomori prefecture.

On the northern frontier, people experimented with paddy agriculture, but any success they met was short-lived, and dry-field production eventually became the system of choice. Rainfall-based agriculture likely included broadcast sowing and the use of wooden spades with iron bits. This form of agriculture continued into recent centuries in Hokkaido, where the Ainu people practiced a mixed economy of agriculture, hunting, fishing, and the gathering of wild plant foods. Soil samples from the Sakushu-Kotoni River site in Sapporo dating to 1300–1100 BP contain the largest collection of cultigen remains yet recovered in Japan. By 1300 BP millet, beans, hemp, barley, wheat, and melons were grown in northern Honshu and Hokkaido. The small number of rice grains found at northern sites suggests that rice was not locally grown but imported.

The wheat grown in Japan until at least the 16th century had the smallest grains ever reported for wheat. Since grain size and plant size are correlated, this wheat plant was also short. Compact wheat is well adapted to regions that experience high winds and heavy rainfalls at harvest time, because the plants will not lodge (become broken by harsh weather). This wheat would have been useful in southern Japan, Korea, and southern China, all of which are monsoonal regions that are frequently exposed to typhoons at harvest time.

THE INDIAN SUBCONTINENT

Research indicates two early stages of agricultural development in South Asia. In the earlier stage, dating roughly from 9500 to 7500 BP, agriculture was being established in parts of Pakistan, in the northwesternmost part of the subcontinent. At the ancient site of Mehrgarh, where the earliest evidence has been found, barley was the dominant crop and was apparently supplemented with some wheat. The barley found there is the well-developed domesticate, six-row barley. A small amount of wild barley and two-row domesticated barley have also been recovered, although archaeologists do not think that barley was independently domesticated in this region. Four types of wheat—einkorn, emmer, durum, and bread wheat—have also been found. All had diffused from Southwest Asia, so it is thought that barley probably did so as well. However, the early barley and wheat in Mehrgarh have predominantly small spherical grains, indicating that varieties adapted to local conditions were developed there. No evidence of irrigation has been found. Goats and sheep were also raised at Mehrgarh at this time.

The second stage, dating to about 7000 BP at Mehrgarh, includes evidence of another crop, cotton. It is quite likely a local domesticate. Other important crops with histories in the Indian subcontinent are mung beans (*Vigna radiata*), black gram (*Vigna mungo*), horsegram (*Macrotyloma uniflorum*), and pigeon pea (*Cajanus cajun*), all of which appear after about 5000 BP. Rice is present by about 7000 BP (and possibly earlier), but in this early period its status as a cultigen is unclear; fully domesticated rice and little millet

(*Panicum sumatrense*) appear in the archaeological record about 4500 BP. Their appearance coincides closely with significant socioeconomic changes in the subcontinent.

Agriculture was well established throughout most of the subcontinent by 6000–5000 BP. During the 5th millennium BP, in the alluvial plains of the Indus River in Pakistan, the cities of Mohenjo-daro and Harappa experienced an apparent explosion of an organized, sophisticated urban culture. This society, known as the Harappan or Indus civilization, flourished until shortly after 4000 BP; it was much more extensive than those of Egypt or Babylonia and appeared earlier than analogous societies in northern China. Harappan society was remarkably homogeneous, thoroughly individual and independent, and a technological peer of the early civilizations of China and Egypt.

Barley and wheat, supplemented by dates, sesame (*Sesamum indicum*), field peas, and lentils, were the primary crops. Goats, sheep, fowl, humped and humpless breeds of Indian cattle (*Bos indicus*), and the Indian elephant (*Elephas maximus*) had been domesticated. In addition to the domestication of a great variety of animals, fragments of dyed and woven cotton fabric attest to the antiquity of the cultivation of cotton plants and of the textile industry for which India was to become famous the world over.

Little archaeological or pictorial evidence of farm implements has survived. It has been surmised, however, that the cereals could have been sown in the fall, on inundated land after the annual flooding of the rivers had receded, and then harvested in spring. Because the system involves minimal skill, labour, and equipment, as the land does not have to be plowed, fertilized, or irrigated, it continues to be used into the 21st century.

The people of the Indus civilization were engaged in a great deal of commerce, and there is proof of river and sea traffic. There was a trading post at Lothal on the Gulf of

Cambay with a brick dockyard and an elaborate channel and spillway. Two-wheeled bullock carts and light covered wagons—forms of transportation that remain common in the early 21st century—were used for local travel. Caravans of pack oxen were the principal mode of transportation over longer distances.

South India, centre of the later distinctive Tamil culture, constituted a second, initially independent agricultural region. Crops were being raised there during the first half of the 4th millennium BP. Two varieties of pulses (legumes) and finger millet (also called *raggee*) were cultivated there.

To the north and west of the Deccan plateau lay a third, intermediate area. There, at Lothal and Rangpur, has been found the earliest South Asian evidence of rice cultivation, in the later Harappan period. Subsequently, wheat, cotton, flax, and lentils spread into the region from the Indus valley, and pulses and millets from the south.

In all three regions the basic cropping pattern of the 4th millennium BP, except the pattern for rice, continued into the 21st century.

EARLY HISTORIC PERIOD

A fourth South Asian agricultural region, the Ganges River valley, became increasingly developed after about 3000 BP. Although it is clear that some of these changes arose from contact with Indo-European speaking peoples known as Aryans, notions of a devastating Aryan invasion are mistaken and in the past tended to obscure objective research on the region's history.

Through various forms of exchange, the region saw the introduction of the horse, coinage, the Brahmi script, and the whole corpus of Vedic texts. Written sources of information join the archaeological sources from this point onward. The plow, for example, figures in a hymn of the most ancient of the texts, the Rigveda:

Harness the plows, fit on the yokes, now that the womb of the earth is ready to sow the seed therein.

Apparently, rice played an important role in the growth of population and the founding of new settlements. These had spread eastward to the Ganges delta by about 2600 BP.

In the later Vedic texts (*c.* 3000–2500 BP) there are repeated references to agricultural technology and practices, including iron implements; the cultivation of a wide range of cereals, vegetables, and fruits; the use of meat and milk products; and animal husbandry. Farmers plowed the soil several times, broadcast seeds, and used a certain sequence of cropping and fallowing. Cow dung provided fertilizer, and irrigation was practiced where necessary.

A more secular eyewitness account is available from Megasthenes (c. 2300 BP), a Greek envoy to the court of the Mauryan empire. In his four-volume Indica, he wrote:

India has many huge mountains which abound in fruit-trees of every kind, and many vast plains of great fertility....The greater part of the soil, moreover, is under irrigation, and consequently bears two crops in the course of the year....In addition to cereals, there grows throughout India much millet...and much pulse of different sorts, and rice also, and what is called bosporum [Indian millet].

And again,

Since there is a double rainfall [i.e., the two monsoons] in the course of each year...the inhabitants of India almost always gather in two harvests annually.

Other sources reveal that the soils and seasons had been classified and meteorological observations of rainfall charted for the different regions of the Mauryan empire, which comprised nearly the whole subcontinent as well as territory to the northwest. A special department of the state supervised the construction and maintenance of the irrigation system, including the dam and conduits at Sudarshana, a human-made lake on the Kathiawar Peninsula. Roads too were the government's responsibility. The swifter horse-drawn chariot provided greater mobility than the bullock cart.

THE MUGHAL CENTURY (C. 1600 CE)

At the climax of the Mughal Empire in the 17th century and with the arrival and presence of the Western powers, a commercial economy based on oceanic trade was evolving. But no technological revolution in cultivating tools or techniques had occurred since roughly the time of the Upanishads (Hindu sacred religious texts, *c.* 2600–2300 BP).

The empire was broadly divided into rice zones and wheat and millet zones. Rice predominated in the eastern states, on the southwest coast, and in Kashmir. Aside from its original home in Gujarat, it had spread also to the Punjab and Sindh with the aid of irrigation. Wheat grew throughout its "natural" region in north and central India. Millets were cultivated in the wheat areas and in the drier districts of Gujarat and Khandesh as well.

Cotton, sugarcane, indigo (*Indigofera* and *Isatis* species), and opium (*Papaver somniferum*) were major cash crops. Cultivation of tobacco, introduced by the Portuguese, spread rapidly. The Malabar Coast was the home of spices, especially black pepper (*Piper nigrum*), that had stimulated the first European adventures in the East. Coffee (*Coffea* species) had been imported from Abyssinia and became a popular beverage in aristocratic circles by the end of the century. Tea, which was to become the commoner's drink and a major export, was yet undiscovered, though it was growing wild in the hills of Assam. Vegetables were culti-vated mainly in the vicinity of towns. New species of fruit, such as the pineapple, papaya, and cashew nut (*Anacardium occidentale*), also were introduced by the Portuguese. The quality of mango and citrus fruits was greatly improved.

Cattle continued to be important as draft animals and for milk. Land use never became as intensive as in China and East Asia, although, as noted by Megasthenes, double (and even triple) cropping was fairly common in regions favoured with irrigation or adequate rainfall. Though the

A well with a Persian wheel near Kolar in Karnataka, India. Universal Images Group/Getty Images

population must have increased many times over since Mauryan times, in the 17th century virgin land was still abundant and peasants were scarce.

Irrigation, however, had greatly expanded. Well water, surface water, and rainwater were captured and stored in tanks, then distributed across the landscape by a network of canals. Some new water-lifting devices—such as the sakia, or Persian wheel, which consists of a series of leather buckets on an endless rope yoked to oxen—had been adopted. All these practices continued to be widely used in the 21st century.

The plow was the principal implement for tillage. Drawn by oxen, the traditional Indian plow has never had a wheel or a moldboard. The part that penetrates the soil is a wedge-shaped block of hardwood. The draft pole projects in front, where it is attached to the neck yoke of the bullocks. A short, upright stilt in the rear serves as a guiding handle. The point of the wedge, to which an iron share may or may not be attached, does not invert the soil. Some plows are so light that the cultivator can carry them daily on his shoulder to and from the fields. Others are heavy, requiring teams of four to six pairs of oxen. Levelers and clod crushers, generally consisting of a rectangular beam of wood drawn by bullocks, are used to smooth the surface before sowing. Among hand tools, the most common is the *kodali*, an iron blade fitted to a wooden handle with which it makes an acute angle.

Drill sowing and dibbling (making small holes in the ground for seeds or plants) are old practices in India. An early 17th-century writer notes that cotton cultivators "push down a pointed peg into the ground, put the seed into the hole, and cover it with earth—it grows better thus." Another simple device was a bamboo tube attached to the plow. The seed was dropped through the tube into the furrow as the plow worked and was covered by the soil in making the next furrow.

Into the 21st century, reaping, threshing, and winnowing continued to be performed almost exactly as described in the Vedic texts. Grain is harvested with a sickle, bound in bundles, and threshed by bullocks treading on it or by hand pounding. To separate the grain from the chaff, it may be sieved with sieves made of stalks of grass or of bamboo, or it may be winnowed by pouring by hand at a height from a *supa* (winnowing scoop). The grain is then measured and stored. The sickle, sieve, and *supa* have remained essentially unchanged over more than two millennia.

SOUTHEAST ASIA

Many crops are native to Southeast Asia, including black pepper, sugarcane (*Saccharum* species), banana (*Musa*

Sweet-potato farming, Southern Highlands province, Papua New Guinea. Bob and Ira Spring

species), nutmeg (*Myristica fragrans*), taro (*Araceae* species), arrowroot (*Maranta* species), coconut (*Arecaceae* species), clove (*Syzygium aromaticum*), yam (*Dioscorea* species), and citrus fruits. The early history of these crops is poorly known. Wild rice (*Zizania* species) is found in the region but was apparently not domesticated there. By 4700–4000 BP, domesticated rice and shell sickles are common at the Khok Phanom Di site in Thailand. It is not known how much earlier domesticated rice was integrated into agriculture in that region. A little rice has been found at Banyan Valley Cave in the Late Hoabinhian. The Hoabinhian is a broad-spectrum foraging culture (having a subsistence strategy similar to that of the American Archaic) dating from the Early Holocene.

New Guinea is another potential area of independent agricultural development in Southeast Asia. In the highland Kuk Swamp site, a long history of land drainage may begin as early as 10,000 BP. Most of the evidence, however, is younger than 6000 BP and consists of a series of drainage channels. There is no agreement on the type of crops grown there.

CHAPTER 4

IMPROVEMENTS IN AGRICULTURE IN THE WEST: 200 BCE TO 1600 CE

Crop farming and domestication of animals were well established in western Europe by the Roman epoch, which began about 200 BCE. Yields per acre were small by 21st-century standards, and nearly half the annual crop had to be used as seed, but quantities of grain were still exported from Britain to Gaul. Where feasible, Roman farming methods were adopted. During the medieval period (roughly the 5th through the 15th century CE), farming practices in the Western world changed radically, first as a result of improvements in agricultural tools and techniques, and later in response to devastating famine, disease, and warfare.

THE ROMAN EPOCH: 200 BCE TO 600 CE

Greek and Roman farming techniques are known from contemporary textbooks that have survived. Methods were dictated to some degree by the Mediterranean climate and by the contours of the area. The majority of the crops cultivated today on the Mediterranean coast—wheat, spelt, barley, some millet, and legumes, including beans, peas, vetch, chickpeas (*Cicer arietinum*), alfalfa (lucerne; *Medicago sativa*), and lupines (*Lupinus* species)—were known at that time. Grapes, olives (*Olea europaea*), radishes (*Raphanus sativus*), turnips (*Brassica* species), and fruit trees were grown.

A mosaic illustrating olive picking in ancient Roman France.
DEA/J. E. Bulloz/De Agostini/Getty Images

THE FARM

Roman holdings were commonly as small as 1.25 acres (0.5 hectare); the ground was prepared with hand tools, hoes, and mattocks, doubtless edged with bronze or iron. Later, as farming developed and estates of different sizes came into existence, two writers set out catalogs of the tools, implements, and labour required to exploit a given-size holding. These were Marcus Porcius Cato (234–149 BCE) and Marcus Terentius Varro (116–27 BCE). Already in Cato's time, emphasis was on production of wine and oil for sale, rather than cultivation of cereal crops, beyond the volume required to feed animals and slaves.

For an olive grove of 240 jugers (150 acres; 60 hectares), Cato estimated necessary equipment as three large carts, six plows and plowshares, three yokes, six sets of ox harness, one harrow, manure hampers and baskets, three packsaddles, and three pads for the asses. Required tools included eight heavy spades, four smaller spades, shovels, rakes, scythes, axes, and wedges. Some 13 people, including an overseer, a housekeeper, five labourers, three teamsters, a muleteer, a swineherd, and a shepherd responsible for 100 sheep, would do the work. Other livestock included three yokes of oxen, three donkeys to carry manure, and one for the olive-crushing mill. The farm was also to be equipped with oil presses and containers for the oil.

FARM IMPLEMENTS

Most Roman-era hand tools were similar in shape to their modern counterparts. The wooden plow was fitted with an iron share and, later, with a coulter (cutter). Though it had no moldboard to turn the soil over, it was sometimes fitted with two small ears that helped to make a more distinct rut. Though it could not turn a furrow, it could invert some of the soil if held sideways. It was usually followed by a man with a mattock who broke up clods and cleared the row so seed would fall into it. Two or three such plowings were given each year to land intended for cereals. Manure was spread only after the second plowing. If spread earlier, it would be buried too deep to do any good. The farm included a compost pit where human and animal excrement were placed along with leaves, weeds, and household waste. Water was added from time to time to rot the mass, and an oak pole was driven into the middle to keep snakes away. Various animal and bird droppings were believed to have different effects on growing plants. Pigeon's dung was valued, but that of aquatic birds was avoided. Marl—earth containing lime, clay, and sand—was used in Gaul and possibly in Britain.

Seeds were sown by hand, broadcast, or dropped. They were covered with a harrow, which may have had iron teeth or may simply have been a thornbush. A more complex plow, fitted with a wheeled forecarriage, may have been used in Cisalpine Gaul (northern Italy) as early as the 1st century CE. Traction normally was supplied by a pair of oxen; the Roman historian Pliny the Elder (23–79 CE) mentions as many as eight being used on heavy land. In light soil, only one was necessary, and sometimes asses were used.

CROPPING SYSTEMS

Olive groves and vineyards were permanent; grain and pulses were annuals. Although it was realized that different soils were better suited to some crops than to others, the same piece of land was used for all crops. A specific crop, however, was grown in alternate years in what is known as the two-field, or crop-and-fallow, system. The fallow land was plowed two or three times during the fallow year to kill the weeds, which typically accumulate where cereal crops are continuously cultivated. Wetland was drained by digging V-shaped trenches, the bottom of which, usually 4 feet (1.2 metres) deep, was paved with loose stones, willow branches, or bundles of brushwood placed lengthwise and covered with the replaced soil. Soil was judged by colour, taste, smell, adhesion to the fingers when rubbed, and whether it filled up a hole from which it had been dug or proved too loose.

Then as now, wheat was mostly sown in autumn, though a species known as *Triticum trimestre* was sometimes planted in spring; it ripened in three months. Barley was a spring-sown crop, as were most others. Though the Romans knew that growing alfalfa and clover was in some way good for the succeeding crop, they did not know why. Similarly, a crop of lupines was sometimes planted for plowing in as green manure, and occasionally a crop of beans was used in the same way.

HARVESTING AND PROCESSING

The harvest was reaped with a curved sickle, a tool that has changed little since Roman times. In some places, the ears of grain were cut and carried in wicker baskets to the threshing floor. The straw was cut and stacked later. In other areas, the plant was cut lower down, and the grain was threshed from the straw. Another set of tools was used, consisting of a short-handled sickle held in the right hand, with the blade at right angles to the handle. A short-handled hooklike implement held in the left hand was used to draw together enough grain to be cut at one stroke. In Gaul a reaper—a cart with an open back pushed by an animal reversed in the shafts—was used. On the edge of the back, a comblike device was fixed to tear off the ears as the vehicle was pushed through the crop. The grain was threshed in the long-established way, by animals treading it on a firm floor, or by an implement known as a *tribulum*, a wooden framework with bits of flint or metal fixed to the underside, hauled over the grain by an animal. Winnowing was still done by tossing in the air from a winnowing basket when there was a favourable wind to blow away the chaff.

Grain was ground with a quern, a hand implement made of two stones, a concave base with a convex upper stone fitted into it. Some querns turned in a circle, while others merely rubbed up and down on the grain. Though designed before the end of the Roman period, water mills were uncommon.

Some forage crops were necessary to feed the plow animals and the cattle, sheep, and pigs. Grass was cut for hay, and many hours must have been spent in the woods collecting acorns for winter feed for the swine. Alfalfa was the best fodder and helped fertility as well. Lupines and a mixed crop of beans, vetch, and chickpeas and another mixture of barley, vetch, and legumes were also employed. Turnips were grown for human and animal consumption in some regions, notably Gaul.

The methods of the Roman farmer produced only limited yields, and cereals were regularly imported to Italy from lands more naturally favourable to grain growing: Egypt, Sicily, Sardinia, and Gaul. Yet the Roman methods were basically sound and, with the help of modern mechanical aids, remain to a large extent in force today.

LIVESTOCK

Little attempt was made at selective breeding, and little was possible, for most of the animals spent their time at open range or in the woods. Nevertheless, different breeds of cattle were recognized as native to particular places.

They were bred between the ages of 2 and 10 years; 2 bulls to 60 or 70 cows was the usual proportion. Greek shepherds garbed some of the very fine-wooled sheep in skin coats to keep their fleece clean. Ewes were bred at three years old, two if essential. They fed on the stubble after harvest. Transhumance, or seasonal migration in search of pasture, was normal. A supply of clear water near the grazing ground was necessary. Goats were kept in large herds, 50 to 100 being the optimum.

Swine were also important. Very fat animals were preferred, and large numbers of these, whose meat was frequently seen on the Roman table, were kept. Sows were covered (bred) at 12 to 20 months of age; it was desirable for them to pig in July or August. The best proportion of boars to sows was 10 to 100. Herds of 100 to 150 ranged the woods. The bacon produced in Gaul had a reputation for quality; swine also flourished in northern Italy and eastern Spain.

THE MEDIEVAL PERIOD: 600 TO 1600 CE

In 1,000 years of medieval history, many details of farming in the Western world changed. The period falls into two divisions: the first, one of development, lasted until the end of the 13th century; the second, a time of recession, was followed by two centuries of recovery.

AGRICULTURAL ADVANCES

The most important agricultural advances took place in the countries north of the Alps, in spite of the large population changes and warfare that accompanied the great migrations and the later onslaughts of Northmen and Saracens. Agriculture had, of course, been practiced regularly in Gaul and Britain and sporadically elsewhere in Europe both before and during the Roman epoch. The climate and soils and, perhaps, the social organization compelled different arrangements of land division and the use of more-complex tools as more and more farmland was converted from forest, marsh, and heath to meet the needs of a rising population.

OPEN-FIELD SYSTEM

The precise origin of the open-field arrangement, which involves long strips of arable land separated from each other by a furrow, balk (ridge of land left after plowing), or mere (boundary), is obscure. The earliest examples of this system date from roughly 800, the year Charlemagne was crowned emperor of the West. Usually these strips of land, normally about 1 acre (0.4 hectare) in size, were laid out in two or three large fields. Each farmer in the village worked a number of these acres; the units forming his holding were scattered among those of other men. The open-field system continued as more land was reclaimed and lasted for many centuries—longer, of course, in some places than in others. It has been suggested that the length of each strip was determined by the distance a draft animal, usually an ox, could haul a plow before stopping for a rest. The intermingling of the strips was said to have been the result of a jointly owned plow team and plow supplied by a number of farmers working together, each being allotted a strip in turn. A subsequent theory holds that in some places the division of fields, which may have originally been rectangular or square, among a number of heirs led to the creation of long, narrow acres. In theory each person's holding totaled 30 acres (12 hectares), comprising strips equally divided between the three arable fields. With the passage of time, wide variations in the size of holdings came about; many became very small.

PLOWS AND PLOWING

Besides the different arrangement of the plowland, there were other changes, some of them important. Though Pliny the Elder claimed a wheeled plow was used in Cisalpine Gaul about the time of Christ, there is a good deal of doubt about that. A wheeled asymmetrical plow was certainly in use in some parts of western Europe by the late 10th century. Illuminated (illustrated) manuscripts and somewhat later calendars show a plow with two wheels fitted with a rudimentary moldboard and a coulter. This plow could invert the soil and turn a true furrow, thus making a better seedbed. Its use left high ridges on the land, traces of which can still be seen in some places.

Medieval farm workers planting seeds on a plowed field.
Hulton Archive/Getty Images

The horse collar, which replaced the old harness band that pressed upon the animal's windpipe, severely restricting its tractive power, was one of the most important inventions in the history of agriculture. Apparently invented in China, the rigid, padded horse collar allowed the animal to exert its full strength, enabling it to do heavier work, plowing as well as haulage. Many peasants continued to use oxen, however, because horses were more expensive to buy and to keep. Some plowing was done by two oxen as in former times; four, eight, or more were occasionally necessary in very difficult land.

HAND TOOLS

Modifications, slight but important, had been introduced into the design of hand tools. A more effective ax made forest clearance easier and faster. The jointed flail supplanted the straight stick. The scythe was more frequently in use for mowing grass, reaping barley, and performing similar tasks. Wind power was applied to the grinding of grain by the earliest windmills. All these changes and adaptations helped expand the cultivated area and supply food for the growing population.

NEW LANDS AND CROPS

Not only were forests cleared and heavy land cultivated, but, in the Netherlands, reclamation from marshland and from the sea was extended. Terps, artificially made patches of higher land on which houses and barns could be built, were made at a very early date in the midst of the marshes. Ditches to drain the fens were dug in the 10th century. Polders, land reclaimed from the sea, are first recorded in the 12th century.

THE WINDMILL

Windmills in Spain. © Goodshoot/Jupiterimages

The windmill is a device for tapping the energy of the wind by means of sails mounted on a rotating shaft. The sails are mounted at an angle or are given a slight twist so that the force of wind against them is divided into two components, one of which, in the plane of the sails, imparts rotation.

Like waterwheels, windmills were among the original prime movers that replaced human beings as a source of power. The use of windmills was increasingly widespread in Europe from the 12th century until the early 19th century. Their slow decline, because of the development of steam power, lasted for a further 100 years. Their rapid demise began following World War I with the development of the internal-combustion engine and the spread of electric power. Interest in wind energy reemerged during the closing decades of the 20th century, but the demands of large-scale electricity generation meant that traditional windmills were supplanted by modern wind turbines.

In Spain the Moors introduced new crops and a new breed of sheep, the Merino, that was to make Spanish wool famous throughout Europe. New crops included sugarcane, rice, cotton, and some subtropical fruits, especially citrus. Grapevines and olive groves flourished in the south, as did the vines the Romans had introduced to the valleys of the Moselle and Rhine rivers. In the 12th century Venice became a major cotton-manufacturing city, processing cotton from the Mediterranean area into cloth for sale in central Europe. Germany also became a cotton-manufacturing centre in the Middle Ages.

Widespread expansion of farmed land occurred throughout western Europe between the 10th century and the later years of the 13th. German and Dutch settlers were encouraged to take up holdings eastward toward the Baltic countries and south to the Carpathians. In France, new villages were built and new farms carved out of the forest, while in England a great deal of land on the boundaries of the open fields was taken in and cultivated. All this new cultivation was carried out with the same old implements and tools; the same crops were cultivated and the same animals bred as before. In remote and desolate places, monastic organizations created great estates. These estates were formed to feed growing populations rather than to improve technical skills. A new literature of farming arose, directed to the attention of great lords and ecclesiastical magnates rather than to the illiterate majority of husbandmen. These bright prospects, however, were dimmed in the 14th century by a combination of calamities.

AGRICULTURAL RECESSION

What is now called a recession began toward the end of the 13th century. The disasters of the 14th—climatic, pestilent, and military—followed. Famine resulted from excessively bad weather in 1314, 1315, and 1316; a small recovery followed in 1317. Yields, never high (from 6 to 10 bushels of wheat per acre [about 500 to 900 litres per hectare] and a little more for barley, rye, and oats), were reduced to nothing by the weather. Floods wiped out the reclaimed land in the Netherlands. Plague followed famine, bringing suffering to both animals and humans. The Black Death broke out in 1347 and is estimated to have killed approximately one-third of the population of Europe. Renewed outbreaks followed throughout the remainder of the century. The Hundred Years' War desolated much of France; other conflicts, accompanied by similar pillage and destruction, broke out elsewhere. The result of all these misfortunes was to be seen in the landscape throughout western Europe. Much of the arable land could not be cultivated for lack of labourers; in some regions the countryside was inhabited by a few scattered peasants grubbing a scanty living in the grimmest isolation. Many of the newer settlements and some of the established ones were abandoned and became deserted villages.

THE NETHERLANDS

The Netherlands was not as seriously affected as most other countries. The flood destruction was repaired, and a system developed that was to become an example to all of Europe. Leguminous and root crops were introduced into the rotation at least as early as the 15th century, and long continuous rotations almost without fallow breaks were employed. Town refuse was added to the supplies of animal manure. The size and milk yield of the Dutch cattle became famous, though possibly exaggerated. Some say that they owed part of their distinction to crosses with animals from Lombardy and Piedmont, which also enjoyed a great reputation. Flemish horses were already renowned for size and strength.

ENGLAND

In England, when agricultural recovery began in the 15th century, there was no immediate improvement in technique. During this period, England became known as the home of most medium- and long-wooled mutton breeds. The profits of the wool trade induced landowners to increase the size of their flocks. This led to some difficulties. Not only had some arable land fallen down to rough grazing because of labour scarcity after the diseases and bad seasons of the 14th century, but the profit of wool encouraged enclosure of formerly open fields for grazing; some villages were even destroyed to increase the area of grazing land. Though there was a considerable outcry against enclosure in the 16th and early 17th centuries, the practice was too profitable to halt. At the same time, farmers began exchanging their scattered plots of land in order to consolidate individual holdings. These consolidated plots were then enclosed with a hedge or fence to prevent them from being subjected to the regulations that governed the use of the remaining strips. Land was also acquired by purchase for this purpose. None of these changes, however, involved any technological advances in farming.

SPAIN

In Spain the shepherds, whose organization, the Mesta, was a powerful body with great political influence, came into conflict with the farmers. The annual journey of sheep from their northern grazing area to the south carried them along an established route; this route steadily broadened, with the sheep trespassing upon the farmers' lands and consuming crops. At the same time, the Mesta successfully opposed any expansion in the amount of arable land until the mid-16th century.

ITALY

In the 14th century the city-states of Italy were devoted to commerce. There was little emphasis on farming, though some attempts at draining marshes were made, and, in spite of the introduction of rice culture in the north, Italian farming on the whole remained much as it had been in Roman times. In the south great flocks were kept and moved up to the mountains for the summer along well-defined paths.

FRANCE

In the 15th century French farmers made substantial progress toward recovery, but even in France there was little advance in technology. The open-field system was prevalent in the north, and a type of Roman farming suited to the environment was practiced in the south, with alfalfa, clover, lupines, and other legumes grown for fodder and to maintain fertility. A fodder crop called Burgundy grass was grown in Burgundy toward the end of the 16th century.

GERMANY

Many of the German villages depopulated by the disasters of the 14th century were never resettled. Some of them had been established on marginal land, such as sandy heaths or places high in the mountains. By the middle of the 16th century, the advanced farming of the Netherlands penetrated into the north at the mouth of the Rhine and in Schleswig-Holstein. This is clear from one of the earliest printed books on farming, by Conrad Heresbach, a German. Heresbach described and recommended many of the methods used by the Romans, including raising lupines for green manure and rotating fallow-manured, winter-sown rape with wheat, rye, and spring barley. For the preparation of the seedbed, the destruction of weeds, manuring, sowing, and harvesting, implements that derived from the Roman pattern were used.

Heresbach's book followed somewhat the pattern of Crescentius, who wrote in the 13th century, and in that respect was similar to the growing number of agricultural treatises that appeared in Spain and France. These were often encyclopaedias of rural life presumably intended for the landowning public. In the late 16th century, Henry IV of France and his minister, Sully, tried to stimulate interest among the lesser nobility in the management of their estates. In England, translations were made of Continental works.

CHAPTER 5
CROP-FARMING CHANGES IN WESTERN EUROPE: 1600 TO 1800

O f the many changes that took place during this period in agricultural history, few were more important than the Norfolk four-course system, characterized by the disappearance of the fallow year and by a new emphasis on fodder crops. The movement toward change was further intensified by the invention of new farm machines, improvements in farm implements, and scientific interest and new biological theories relating to farm and animal life.

THE NORFOLK FOUR-COURSE SYSTEM

Established in Norfolk county, England, and in several other counties before the end of the 17th century, the so-called Norfolk four-course system involved a strict rotation of crops over a four-year period. Wheat was grown in the first year, followed by turnips in the second, then barley, with clover and ryegrass undersown, in the third. The clover and ryegrass were grazed or cut for feed in the fourth year. The turnips were either employed for feeding cattle in open yards during the winter (some covered yards were built) or for feeding sheep confined in folds set up on the ground. This new system was cumulative in effect, for the fodder crops eaten by the livestock produced large supplies of previously scarce animal manure, and that was richer in nature because the animals were better fed.

When the sheep grazed the fields, their urine and droppings fertilized the soil, so that heavier cereal yields were obtained in following years.

The Norfolk four-course system became fairly general on the newly enclosed farms by 1800, remaining almost standard practice on most British farms for the best part of the following century. The system was used in the Lothians and some other parts of Scotland by about 1800. During the first three-quarters of the 19th century, it was adopted in much of continental Europe.

ENCLOSURE

In order to adopt the Norfolk four-course system, it was first necessary to alter the thousand-year-old layout of the arable fields. It was virtually impossible for an individual farmer to grow fodder crops on his strips of land in open fields, for at certain seasons (after harvest, for example) these fields were opened to grazing by the livestock of the whole community. The improving farmer, who grew clover and ryegrass or other legumes or a root crop, would simply have provided additional feed for his neighbours' as well as his own animals. Such an arrangement was possible, of course, if all the farmers cooperated, a rather unlikely but not absolutely unknown state of affairs. On enclosed land, however, a farmer could cultivate these crops and benefit from his own efforts.

Consequently there was a rapid acceleration of the enclosure movement in England, sometimes by local agreement, by Chancery decree (late 17th century), and by private acts of Parliament in growing numbers (18th century). Some 6 million acres (some 2.4 million hectares) of English fields were enclosed between 1700 and 1845. On the European continent, the change, where it was made, took place slightly later. Some farms are still worked in strips, though communal regulation has vanished.

LIVESTOCK

Where new fodder crops were introduced into the rotation, more and better livestock were bred and kept. Animal size increased, and meat development was greater. In cows, milk yield improved. Better breeding increased fleece and flesh production in sheep and improved the size of pigs. Horses, essential to transport, were carefully bred. There were disastrous outbreaks of cattle plague, however, that spread throughout Europe in the second and fourth decades of the 18th century, possibly introduced from eastern Europe by cattle driven to markets in the west. As a result of these calamities, a veterinary school was founded at Lyon, in 1762, and a second at Alfort, France,

Merino sheep grazing in Spain. Jose Antonio Moreno/ age fotostock/Getty Images

in 1767. Denmark established its first veterinary school in 1773, and England followed in 1791.

An interesting aspect of livestock breeding was the admiration of all Europe for the Spanish Merino sheep, which were forbidden from export for fear of competition. It proved impossible to maintain the prohibition. Merinos were obtained by Louis XVI of France in 1786. Some had been imported into Sweden even earlier, before 1765. Both Prussia and Saxony raised them by midcentury, the Saxon Merino becoming famous. Austria also secured Merinos, and George III of England had obtained a few by the end of the century. Merinos were not a success in England, however.

Though a major source of meat since Roman times, pigs had been raised half wild, feeding in the woods under the care of a swineherd and his dogs. Over a large part of western Europe, this system continued, especially where open-field farming prevailed. In England, however, where population doubled during the 18th century from about 5 million to about 10 million, more care was taken in breeding productive swine. Several different breeds could already be distinguished; some were crossed with Chinese animals possibly transported in vessels carrying spices and tea.

IMPROVEMENTS IN TECHNOLOGY

The 17th and 18th centuries were marked by significant technological advancement in European agriculture. New farm equipment and methods of land management both facilitated production and enabled farmers to raise a wider variety of crops and livestock. Such strides stimulated commercial agricultural activity, which, in turn, spurred publication of farming literature as well as the establishment of various agricultural societies.

PLOWS AND FARM MACHINERY

Probably of Dutch origin, the Rotherham plow, the main design of which has remained virtually unchanged to this day, was first put into use in the Netherlands, England, and Scotland during the first half of the 18th century. Details of design varied from area to area. Some Rotherham plows were wheeled, and some were not; some were made of timber; others of iron. The first factory for making plows was established in England in 1783.

Though the problem of mechanizing harvest work was not solved until the 19th century, a few fairly simple threshing machines had been designed and put in use by 1800. Similarly, a variety of machines for such tasks as preparing animal feed, chopping turnips, and cutting chaff were designed and used.

The English gentleman Jethro Tull (1674–1741) made important contributions during this period, among them the horse-drawn hoe and the seed drill. To save expensive hand labour, Tull designed and fabricated horse-drawn hoes that destroyed the weeds and kept the soil between the rows in good crumbly (friable) condition. Tull believed that friable soil would supply all the nutrients a plant required, and he was so convinced of his theory that he planted wheat in rows spaced widely enough to allow for horse hoeing while the plant was growing. Tull also believed that placing the seed into the ground in small holes (drilling) would permit a much lighter rate of seeding than hand broadcast methods while still obtaining high yields. To place the seeds, he designed and used a seed drill.

Tull was not the first man to invent a seed drill. A seed dropper, consisting of a tube attached to a plow through which seed could be dropped by hand at regular intervals, had been attached to an ancient Babylonian plow. A similar system, but with two tubes behind two plowshares

THE PLOW

The plow, or plough, can be considered the most important agricultural implement since the beginning of history. The device is used to turn and break up soil and to bury crop residues. It also helps to control weeds.

A tractor pulling a disk plow. Courtesy of John Deere

The antecedent of the plow is the prehistoric digging stick. The earliest plows were doubtless digging sticks fashioned with handles for pulling or pushing. By Roman times, light, wheelless plows with iron shares (blades) were drawn by oxen; these implements could break up the topsoil of the Mediterranean regions but could not handle the heavier soils of northwestern

A tractor pulling a large chisel plow. Courtesy of John Deere

Europe. The wheeled plow, at first drawn by oxen but later by horses, made possible the northward spread of European agriculture. The 18th-century addition of the moldboard, which turned the furrow slice cut by the plowshare, was an important advance. In the mid-19th century the black prairie soils of the American Midwest challenged the strength of the existing plow, and American mechanic John Deere invented the all-steel one-piece share and moldboard. The three-wheel sulky plow followed and, with the introduction of the gasoline engine, the tractor-drawn plow.

set in a rectangular frame, was employed in 17th-century China, and probably at a very much earlier date. An Italian described a modern form of seed drill in the late 16th century. An Austrian, Joseph von Locatelli, described a *sembrador*, or seed drill attached to a plow, which was either used or proposed for use in Spain. After Tull, inventors were numerous, and, at the end of the 18th century, the drilling of seed, though not commonplace, was accepted. Throughout this period, however, the ordinary farmer continued to prepare his seedbed by plowing three times a year, occasionally more, and broadcasting seed by hand and harrowing it in. All these techniques were thousands of years old.

IRRIGATION AND DRAINAGE

Walter Blith, a captain in Oliver Cromwell's army, was interested in land drainage and irrigation in the form of water meadows, pieces of low, flat land capable of being kept in fertility by being overflowed from some adjoining stream. During his lifetime considerable drainage work was carried out in eastern England, where it has continued to the present day. At the same time, water meadows were constructed in southwest England. This system was well known and of long standing in Germany. Similarly, there were sporadic attempts to drain wetlands in France and Italy; maintenance of the drainage system was essential to parts of the Netherlands. Colonization of reclaimed lands in eastern England by Dutch settlers also introduced some novel crops to that area, especially rape and cole.

IMPORTANCE OF THE AMERICAS

The age of exploration that began in the mid-15th century led to discovery of edible plants and animals previously unknown to Europeans. Arabs had introduced sugarcane and rice to some parts of southern Europe. The voyagers to North America returned with corn, tobacco, and the turkey. South America supplied the potato, cocoa, quinine, and some vegetable drugs, while coffee, tea, and indigo came from the East.

Though the tropical plants could not be cultivated in the temperate European climate, corn was rapidly adopted in southern Europe. Imported first to Ireland, the potato came into general use elsewhere by the end of the 18th century.

These novel crops expanded the dietary range in some places, and importation of the new beverages may have helped reduce the very large consumption of alcoholic drinks. Tea drinking was regarded as harmful by some fervent propagandists at the end of the 17th century and later, and, in the 1820s, the English popular journalist William Cobbett even condemned the potato. By that time, however, the crop had become the staple food of the Irish rural population and was raised on a moderate scale in Lancashire and Cheshire for consumption by their growing manufacturing population, as it was in some parts of Germany, France, the Low Countries, and Italy.

In the 16th and 17th centuries the introduction of sheep into the Americas—notably such countries as Argentina, with suitable climate and grazing land—proved highly successful.

AGRICULTURAL TEXTBOOKS AND IMPROVEMENT SOCIETIES

The small number of vernacular farming textbooks printed in Europe during the 16th century increased in the 17th and became much larger in the 18th, indicating a developing interest in commercial farming. Population growth, especially in the urban centres, and the rise of industry opened new opportunities for the enterprising landlord and farmer, even though transport was difficult. English writers on farming were more numerous than those in other countries. The French paid more attention to gardening, and the Thirty Years' War (1618–48) brought a long interruption in agricultural development in Germany and adjacent countries.

The Flemish and Dutch produced no agricultural texts, declaring that they were more interested in farming than in writing about it. Indeed, the system of crop rotation in Brabant and Flanders became the pattern for the rest of Europe. In 1645 an Englishman, Sir Richard Weston, wrote the first description of this system, which featured crops such as clover or roots, rotating with industrial crops such as flax, with no fallow break. Adoption in England and other parts of western Europe increased agricultural production between 1600 and 1800.

The problem of educating the ordinary farmer occupied the minds of improving landlords who were the governing class in every European country. Improvement societies formed in Great Britain, and a semiofficial Board of Agriculture, financed in part by a government grant, was established there in 1793. It lasted until 1822. One of the first tasks it undertook was to make and publish a survey of each county in the kingdom in order to make the best local methods known to other districts. A similar plan had been tried in France in 1759. Other countries in western Europe engaged in similar activities. A Royal Society was established in Denmark in 1769 and made practical researches. The Italian Società di Georgofili, founded in 1753, tried to stimulate technical improvement and planned large drainage schemes. The first similar Swiss society was established at Zürich in 1747. Frederick William I of Germany founded an agricultural school at Halle in 1727; and the first agricultural high school was begun, with royal encouragement, at Möglin, near Berlin, in 1806.

PROGRESS IN DIFFERENT COUNTRIES

Despite the advancements in agricultural techniques, progress in the various countries of Europe was uneven. Germany, for instance, readily adopted the new methods, and agriculture flourished. Spain, by contrast, adhered to its older traditions and, consequently, did not see a remarkable increase in production.

ITALY

Although Italy was the first country where a four-course rotation was advocated, traditional farming persisted there into the 18th century and even later. Italian farmers, however, had accepted corn, potatoes, tomatoes, and tobacco and relied upon these and other subtropical products for subsistence and sale. The vine continued to be important, as did the olive. The north was more advanced than the less fertile south; a wide variety of crops was grown there, often in long rotations with a reduction of the proportion of fallow. An occasional fodder crop of turnips, clover, and ryegrass was cultivated. Shortages of fodder encouraged adoption of the Norfolk four-course system. Plows and other implements, however, remained primitive. The mulberry tree, the leaves of which provided food for silkworms, was important in the Milanese and Piedmont area. Rice was also grown on irrigated land in that area. High-yielding milk cows were also kept. Transhumance was practiced, with sheep on the lower lands in winter and on the mountain pastures in summer.

SPAIN

Spain retained farming traditions rooted in the past, partly because of its physical and climatic conditions and partly from social pressure. The Merino sheep, fine horses, and mules continued to deserve their high repute. Some subtropical crops were cultivated in the south and east—sugarcane, cotton, grapes, olives, figs, raisins, and oranges—but the arid and stony land of the centre and elsewhere remained substantially unproductive and thinly populated by a poor class of métayers (sharecroppers).

BRITAIN

The Industrial Revolution in Great Britain drew many people from food production; this had happened before in the mercantile and manufacturing Low Countries. Since these people still had to be fed, there existed a strong incentive toward increased farm productivity. These countries could not, however, satisfy local demands, and they sought to import food, especially grain. Thus, industrialization in England stimulated cereal growing in Prussia, Poland, and parts of Russia.

GERMANY

Increased grain production in Prussia was also stimulated by the personal efforts of Frederick II (Frederick the Great), who set out to repair some of the damage caused by the Thirty Years' War and generally to improve conditions in his country. He ordered the rearrangement of the open-field farms into separate enclosed holdings and did away with common grazing, doubtless to encourage better animal selection and breeding. He bred horses for the army and gave bulls and rams to favoured landowners. Elsewhere in the German congeries of small states, the princes enforced improvements by royal edicts. Fodder crops were introduced. In addition to keeping the animals indoors in winter, summer stall feeding was introduced

Frederick II. Imagno/Hulton Archive/Getty Images

in some areas, resulting in preservation of the animal manure formerly dropped on the commons.

Sugar beets had been grown for feed in Germany, but it was not until 1747 that sugar was successfully extracted and not until 1802 that the first factory for making beet sugar was built. This industry, however, did not really begin to grow until the time of the Napoleonic Wars.

SCANDINAVIA

The countries of Scandinavia were influenced by the spirit of improvement, but less spectacularly. Danish farmers were somewhat hindered in the introduction of novel methods by political restrictions, and it was not until the end of the 19th century that serious advances in technique took place. Sweden had some improvers who imported Merino sheep, English cattle, and Angora goats and who studied plow design. Nevertheless, Swedish farming in general remained almost static until after 1757, when some exchange of strips made enclosed farms possible. Potatoes became a staple.

NORTH AMERICA

Changes in farming technique that increased productivity, introduced primarily in Great Britain and the Netherlands before 1800, made British farming the example to the world, even the distant lands of America. That continent, north and south, had indeed supplied Europe with very valuable plants. By the end of the 18th century, the production of North America was sufficient to supply some of the necessities of a warring Europe. The New England settlements, like those of the Southern states, were expanding toward the west, as land was claimed from the forest. Agriculture produced small surpluses for export. The Southern states had, of course, always exported staples like tobacco, cotton, and (Louisiana) sugar; but the processes by which these plants were cultivated remained primitive.

Cattle raising expanded rapidly in the Americas. The need for fresh and larger grazing areas drew cattle farming west into Ohio and Kentucky, where corn for fattening purposes could be raised at low cost. Cattle were being driven overland to seaboard markets by 1805.

CHAPTER 6

THE 19TH-CENTURY POWER REVOLUTION ON THE FARM: c. 1792 TO 1914

The development of agriculture between the close of the 18th century and the early years of the 20th century was characterized by the partial mechanization of agriculture in western Europe—especially in Great Britain—and in the previously untapped lands of Australia, New Zealand, and North America, where wild, uncultivated, and virtually unoccupied land was made to yield vast quantities of plant and animal crops.

MECHANIZATION

Though the first steps had been taken earlier, it was not until after 1850 that mechanization took hold in western Europe and the newly settled countries. A variety of machines were slowly coming into use when the French revolutionary wars broke out in the 1790s. An efficient seed drill had been devised but still required demonstration in the 1830s to convince farmers of its value. A few threshing machines were in use before 1800, and they became steadily more popular until, in the 1830s, farm labourers in England rebelled against them because the machine robbed them of their winter employment. The speed with which the thresher was adopted is rather surprising, as there was a surplus rather than a shortage of labour at the time.

THE REAPER

Yet even an ample supply of labour could not always cope with the harvest by hand methods. Local labour frequently had to be supplemented by traveling gangs or by small tradesmen from neighbouring towns. This unsatisfactory situation proved an incentive to invention. Reaping machines had been proposed before, but not until Patrick Bell in Scotland and Cyrus Hall McCormick in the United States produced their designs did this machine become a practical reality. After the Great Exhibition of London in

An illustration of a McCormick reaper being used during a harvest. Stock Montage/Archive Photos/Getty Images

1851, the reaper slowly came into general use. About this time an animal-pushed combine harvester, which stripped the grain from the plant like the Gallo-Roman reaper of classical times, was devised. This machine was used successfully in South Australia, where more grain was grown than could be harvested manually by the few labourers available there.

PLOWS AND PLOWING

Before harvesting machines could be used, however, the ground had to be prepared, and the fundamental instrument for this purpose was the plow. Though attempts had been made in the 17th and 18th centuries to develop a mathematical theory of plow design, in a less esoteric way practical men had made significant improvements. Prominent among these was the English inventor Robert Ransome, who patented a cast-iron share in 1785 and a self-sharpening share in 1803. Later he designed a plow with standard parts that could be removed and replaced in the field, a double plow (i.e., with two shares), and other patterns.

As settlers in the United States moved westward, plowing of the black prairie soils, high in organic matter, posed a special problem to the farmers who had cast-iron and iron-patched plows. The ingenuity of John Deere, an Illinois blacksmith and plow maker of the 1830s, resulted in a new kind of plow that was made entirely of steel except for the braces, beam, and handles. The one-piece share and moldboard of his first steel plow was cut from a mill-saw blade and shaped over a wooden form. This greatly improved implement not only made possible the effective plowing of the black prairie soils but also considerably lessened the animal power needed to turn the soil.

A mole plow, characterized by a cartridge-shaped "mole" attached to the bottom of its wide cutting blade, and intended for plowing a drain in heavy wetland, was successfully fabricated and used in the late 18th century. The plow, pulled by a capstan or team of animals, was a great help in draining wetlands. Invention of a method for manufacturing tubular clay pipes also aided and simplified drainage. Use of these pipes spread rapidly beginning about 1850; large areas of land were thus drained all over Europe. Drainage by this method continues today.

STEAM-POWERED EQUIPMENT

The first attempts at steam-powered plowing took place in the 1830s. Though ingenious, the early apparatus was impractically heavy and cumbersome. A successful steam plow was made in the 1860s, after which steam power was widely adopted, especially on large farms. Supplementary implements helpful to the farmer were also produced about this time. They include hay rakes, hay-loaders, and potato spinners. Barn machinery, housed in specially designed buildings, was driven by a steam engine through a system of belts and pulleys or in less mechanized style by horses. Threshing drums and supplementary machines were often hauled about the countryside by steam traction engines and worked on a contract basis by itinerant gangs of agricultural labourers.

Steam power spread rapidly but thinly over Europe. The first steam plow was worked in the Netherlands in 1862. Though milking machines were built, they were not really successful until the end of the century. The cream separator and milk cooler, both little changed since the time of their invention, were introduced in the 1880s.

Progress in mechanization in the second half of the 19th century was not, of course, confined to agriculture.

Transport and communications improved enormously. Steamships facilitated the movement of goods and the spread of ideas. Railroads were built throughout the world, making agriculture possible in areas where farmers previously had no way to carry their goods to market. The first shipment of cattle marketed by rail originated in Lexington, KY., in 1852. These cattle were driven to Cincinnati, Ohio, freighted to Cleveland on Lake Erie, boated to Buffalo, freighted to Albany, N.Y., and then boated down the Hudson River to New York City. By 1860 railroads had extended beyond the Mississippi River, opening the Southwest to range production and the Midwest to cattle feeding.

APPLYING SCIENCE TO FARMING

Mechanical developments in the 19th century were paralleled by scientific discovery. Research in plant physiology and nutrition begun in the 18th century continued and grew in scope. While scientists developed new fertilizers to increase overall farm productivity, they also sought means to make crops more resistant to disease.

NEW FERTILIZERS

In 1813 the brilliant English chemist Sir Humphry Davy summarized the current state of agricultural knowledge in a series of lectures published as *Elements of Agricultural Chemistry*. Though Davy's lectures probably had little impact on the ordinary farmer, a few enterprising pioneers were soon conducting field experiments with new fertilizers. The beneficial effects of saltpetre (potassium nitrate) had been known since the 17th century. When a firm began to import saltpetre from India in the 1820s, interested farmers bought and used it. Imported Chilean nitrate of soda was more plentiful, however, and more often used. Peruvian guano, an organic fertilizer, was imported and extensively used, even though sellers often diluted it with useless material to increase its bulk. Ground bones and other kinds of waste had been used in the late 18th century for restoring phosphate to pastures in dairy areas. Perhaps it was the use of these bones and their cracking and soaking in sulfuric acid that led to the production of superphosphate of lime in the 1840s. As the 19th century continued, more mineral fertilizers were discovered and marketed. With the development of the chemical industry, other fertilizers were manufactured. Basic slag, a waste product of the iron industry, was applied to grasslands with success. Gypsum was also tried but was later superseded by more effective products.

Humphry Davy. Hulton Archive/ Getty Images

AGRICULTURAL RESEARCH AND EDUCATION

Scientists of the 18th century had established the principles that governed plant life. About 1837 the English agriculturist Sir John Bennet Lawes began to experiment with the effects of manures on plants and crops. In 1842 he patented a process for treating phosphate rock to produce superphosphate and thus initiated the synthetic fertilizer industry. In the following year Lawes enlisted the services of the English scientist J.H. (later Sir Henry) Gilbert, with whom he worked for more than half a century, performing experiments on crop and animal nutrition. The work of Rothamsted Experimental Station, which Lawes founded and endowed, became world renowned. At the same time, similar work was carried out in France, Germany, and the United States.

Though a considerable number of books on agricultural subjects appeared during the 19th century, their effect was perhaps less than that of the measures taken to promote agricultural education in most European countries. Though schools for farmers had been established in some German states in the 18th century, the first professorships of rural agriculture and economy were established at Oxford (1790) and Edinburgh (1797). Though similar events took place in France and Germany in the 19th century, a key date in the history of agricultural research and education is 1862, when the U.S. Congress set up the Department of Agriculture and provided for colleges of agricultural and mechanical arts in each state.

DISEASE

An important spur to research was the great prevalence of plant disease, which at intervals became epidemic. Two crops—the potato and the grapevine—were virulently attacked in the 1840s, and irreparable damage resulted. When the potato blight struck Ireland, where the potato was a staple food crop, it caused widespread famine. The vine growers of southern Europe suffered several disastrous epidemics of the vine fungus. Later in the century,

LATE BLIGHT

The water mold *Phytophthora infestans* causes late blight, a disease that affects potato and tomato plants. The disease occurs in humid regions with temperature ranges between 40° and 80° F (4° and 29° C); hot, dry weather checks its spread. Potato or

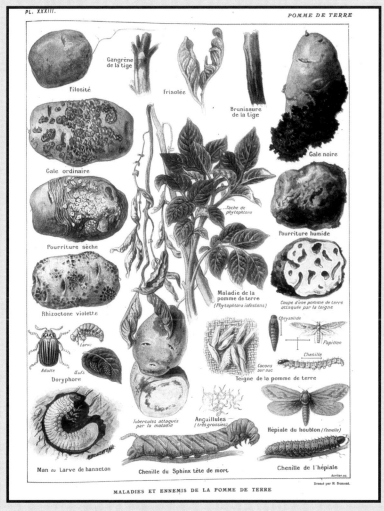

A chart showing various diseases that can affect potatoes. Late blight, or Phytophthora infestans, *is shown towards the centre.* Universal Images Group/Getty Images

tomato vines that are infected may rot within two weeks. The Irish potato famines of the mid-19th century were caused by late blight. The disease destroyed more than half of the tomato crop in the eastern United States in 1946, leading to the establishment of a blight-forecasting service in 1947.

When plants have become infected, lesions (round or irregularly shaped areas that range in colour from dark green to purplish black and resemble frost injury) appear on the leaves, petioles, and stems. A whitish growth of spore-producing structures may appear at the margin of the lesions on the underleaf surfaces. Potato tubers develop rot up to 0.6 inch (15 mm) deep. Secondary fungi and bacteria (*Erwinia* species) often invade potato tubers and produce rotting that results in great losses during storage, transit, and marketing.

infestation by the vine louse grape phylloxera nearly put an end to European viticulture.

FARMING OUTSIDE EUROPE

In the 19th century, European colonial expansion and plantation farming spread to many areas of the world. Products such as coffee, tea, and sugarcane were grown extensively in the colonies with tropical climates. The temperate regions were found to be best suited for meat and dairy farming as well as grain production.

EUROPEAN COLONIES

Coffee was grown widely in Sri Lanka until disease destroyed the plants and they were replaced by tea bushes. Sugarcane was raised on a large scale in the East and West Indies, in the United States, and the Hawaiian Islands. Cocoa was carried from South America to colonies in

West Africa, where it prospered. Natural rubber was tapped in the Congo region and Brazil and was later cultivated in well-designed plantations in the Malay Peninsula. Palm oil was collected from trees in West Africa and the South Sea islands. Yet these spectacular developments had little impact on the native agriculture of the underdeveloped regions in general; ancient patterns of cultivation remained largely unchanged.

THE UNITED STATES AND AUSTRALIA

By 1900 much of the western United States had been settled; great livestock ranches and wheat farms had been established there and in Argentina. A large dairy and sheep industry had grown up in Australia and New Zealand. Imported Merinos were the foundation stock of the vast flocks that grazed the Australian hinterland. Devon cattle were exported from England to South Africa, where sheep were also a significant economic factor.

The Great Plains of the United States, lying between the Mississippi River and the Rocky Mountains, were first used by the open-range cattle industry, the heyday of which lasted from about 1866 to 1886. To improve their lean, lanky longhorn, breeders imported Herefords, Durham Shorthorns, and other fine European cattle. As the range became more and more heavily occupied, and as wheat farmers began to till the soil of the Great Plains, it became necessary to put up fences. This was accomplished with a remarkable invention, barbed wire, a new, cheap, and rapidly erected kind of fencing, used in preference to the post and rail fences or the sod and stone walls that had been common in Europe for centuries.

Grain farmers rapidly followed the ranchers, and farming spread from Oklahoma north into Canada. Because hand labour was scarce, cultivation and harvesting were rapidly mechanized. A combine harvester hauled by a large team of mules was used in California in the late 1880s. Different from the combine harvester used in South Australia, this was a prototype of the contemporary combine. Iron and steel plows were produced in large numbers, and steam traction engines were used as power units for many mechanized operations such as threshing. Though seed was usually drilled, yields were often low because manure was in short supply. Furthermore, with manure scarce, a three-year rotation was practiced to prevent soil depletion: two crop plantings were followed by a fallow year. In the Southern states, export staples were produced in addition to subsistence crops.

America's prodigious new supplies of meat and grain were generally exported from the wide ranges of the Western states to the more populous Eastern states and to Europe, where they lowered prices paid to European farmers but played an important role in feeding populations in industrial centres. Fresh meat and dairy produce from Argentina and Australia were carried thousands of miles in newly developed refrigerator ships.

The huge quantities of inexpensive food produced by the newly settled countries created a difficult problem for the European farmer. The arable and mixed farming common in most European countries simply could not compete. In Great Britain, much cropland was planted with grass, and farmers began to raise pedigree animals and dairy produce. On the Continent, where many farmers occupied peasant holdings, a kind of subsistence farming continued. Denmark and the Netherlands turned to production of dairy produce and high-quality bacon, feeding pigs on waste dairy materials.

CHAPTER 7

THE 20TH CENTURY: NEW MACHINES, CROPS, AND FARMING TECHNIQUES

Agricultural technology developed more rapidly in the 20th century than in all previous history. Though the most important developments during the first half of the century took place in the industrial countries, especially the United States, the picture changed somewhat after the 1950s. With the coming of independence, former colonies in Africa and Asia initiated large-scale efforts to improve their agriculture. In many cases they used considerable ingenuity in adapting Western methods to their own climates, soils, and crops.

DEVELOPMENTS IN POWER: THE INTERNAL-COMBUSTION ENGINE

The internal-combustion engine brought major changes to agriculture in most of the world. In advanced regions it soon became the chief power source for the farm.

THE TRACTOR

The first applications to agriculture of the four-stroke-cycle gasoline engine were as stationary engines, at first in Germany, later elsewhere. By the 1890s stationary engines were mounted on wheels to make them portable, and soon a drive was added to make them self-propelled. The first successful gasoline tractor was built in the United States in 1892. Within a few years several companies were manufacturing tractors in Germany, the United Kingdom, and the United States. The number of tractors in the more developed countries increased dramatically during the 20th century, especially in the United States: in 1907 some 600 tractors were in use, but the figure had grown to almost 3.4 million by 1950.

Major changes in tractor design throughout the 20th century produced a much more efficient and useful machine. Principal among these were the power takeoff, introduced in 1918, in which power from the tractor's engine could be transmitted directly to an implement through the use of a special shaft; the all-purpose, or tricycle-type, tractor (1924), which enabled farmers to cultivate planted crops mechanically; rubber tires (1932), which facilitated faster operating speeds; and the switch to four-wheel drives and diesel power in the 1950s and 1960s, which greatly increased the tractor's pulling power. The last innovations led to the development of enormous tractors—often having double tires on each wheel and enclosed, air-conditioned cabs—that can pull several gangs of plows. By the 21st century, tractors were benefiting from ever increasing power as well as from Global Positioning System (GPS) satellite navigation systems.

UNIT MACHINERY

After World War II, there was an increase in the use of self-propelled machines in which the motive power and the equipment for performing a particular task formed one unit. Though the grain combine is the most important of these single-unit machines, self-propelled units are also in use for spraying, picking cotton, baling hay, picking corn, and harvesting tomatoes, lettuce, sugar beets, and many other crops. These machines are faster, easier to operate, and above all, have lower labour requirements than those that are powered by a separate tractor.

GRAIN COMBINES

The first successful grain combine, a machine that cuts ripe grain and separates the kernels from the straw, was built in the United States in 1836. Lack of an adequate power unit and the tendency of combined grain to spoil because of excessive moisture limited its development, however. Large combines, powered by as many as 40 horses, were used in California in the latter part of the 19th century. Steam engines replaced horses on some units as a power source, but, about 1912, the gasoline engine began to replace both horses and steam for pulling the combine and operating its mechanism. A one-man combine, powered by a two-plow-sized tractor (i.e., one large enough to pull two plows), was developed in 1935. This was followed by a self-propelled machine in 1938.

MECHANIZED EQUIPMENT FOR CORN

Corn (maize), the most important single crop in the United States and extremely important in many other countries, is grown commercially with the aid of equipment operated by tractors or by internal-combustion engines mounted on the machines. Maize pickers came into use in the U.S. Corn Belt after World War I and were even more widely adopted after World War II. These pickers vary in complexity from the snapper-type harvester, which removes the ears from the stalks but does not husk them, to the picker-sheller, which not only removes the husk but shells the grain from the ear. The latter is often used in conjunction with dryers. Modern machines can harvest as many as 12 rows of corn at a time.

THE COMBINE

Combine funneling harvested wheat into a truck. Comstock Images/Thinkstock

The combine is a complex farm machine that both cuts and threshes grain. In design, it is essentially a binder-type cutting device that delivers the grain to a threshing machine modified to work as it moves across the field. The cutting–gathering component, designed to take the grain with a minimum of straw, is sometimes called the header. A threshing cylinder rubs grain out of the heads against a concave surface. Some grain and chaff go with the straw to the straw deck, on which grain is shaken out and delivered to the cleaning shoe. Some of the grain and chaff go directly to the cleaning shoe, on which sieves and a blast of air are used to separate and clean the grain. After passing through the air blast, the grain drops into a clean-grain auger that conveys it to an elevator and into a storage tank. Straw drops out of the back of the combine in a windrow for baling or is scattered over the ground by a fanlike spreader. Some combines for use on steeply rolling land have a body supported in a frame by hydraulic cylinders that automatically adjust to keep the body level.

MECHANIZED EQUIPMENT FOR COTTON

Mechanization has also reduced substantially the labour needed to grow cotton. Equipment includes tractor, two-row stalk-cutter, disk (to shred the stalks), bedder (to shape the soil into ridges or seedbeds), planter, cultivator, sprayer, and harvester. Cotton fibre is harvested by a stripper-type harvester, developed in the 1920s, or by a picker. The stripper strips the entire plant of both open and unopened bolls and collects many leaves and stems. Though a successful cotton picker that removed the seed cotton from the open bolls and left the burrs on the plant was invented in 1927, it did not come into use until after World War II. Strippers are used mostly in dry regions, while pickers are employed in humid, warm areas. The pickers are either single-row machines mounted on tractors or two-row self-propelled machines.

TOMATO-HARVESTING EQUIPMENT

The self-propelled mechanical tomato harvester, developed in the early 1960s by engineers working in cooperation with plant breeders, handles virtually all packing tomatoes grown in California. Harvesters using electronic sorters can further reduce labour requirements.

AUTOMOBILES, TRUCKS, AND AIRPLANES

The automobile and truck have also had a profound effect upon agriculture and farm life. Since their appearance on American farms between 1913 and 1920, trucks have changed patterns of production and marketing of farm products. Trucks deliver such items as fertilizer, feed, and fuels; go into the fields as part of the harvest equipment; and haul the crops to markets, warehouses, or packing and processing plants. Most livestock is trucked to market.

The airplane may have been used agriculturally in the United States as early as 1918 to distribute poison dust over cotton fields that were afflicted with the pink boll-worm. While records of this experiment are fragmentary, it is known that airplanes were used to locate and map cotton fields in Texas in 1919. In 1921 a widely publicized dusting experiment took place near Dayton, Ohio. Army pilots, working with Ohio entomologists, dusted a 6-acre (2.5-hectare) grove of catalpa trees with arsenate of lead to control the sphinx caterpillar. The experiment was successful, and it, along with others, encouraged the development of dusting and spraying, mainly to control insects, disease, weeds, and brush. In recognition of the possible long-term harmful effects of some of the chemicals, aerial dusting and spraying have been subject to various controls since the 1960s.

Airplanes are also used to distribute fertilizer, to reseed forest terrain, and to control forest fires. Many rice growers use planes to seed, fertilize, and spray pesticides, and even to hasten crop ripening by spraying hormones from the air.

During heavy storms, airplanes have dropped baled hay to cattle stranded in snow. Airplanes have also been used to transport valuable breeding stock, particularly in Europe. Valuable and perishable farm products are frequently transported by air. Airplanes are especially valuable in such large agricultural regions as western Canada and Australia, where they provide almost every type of service to isolated farmers.

NEW CROPS AND TECHNIQUES

New crops and techniques are, in reality, modifications of the old. Soybeans, sugar beets, and grain sorghums, for example, all regarded as "new" crops, are new only in the sense that they are now grown in wider areas and have different uses from those of earlier times. Such techniques as terracing, dry farming, and irrigation are nearly as old as the practice of agriculture itself, but their widespread application is still increasing productivity in many parts of the world.

NEW CROPS

In the 20th century Asian soybeans, West African sorghum, and sugar beets from Europe rose from relative regional obscurity to become major crops on a worldwide scale. All of these crops were cultivated on multiple continents. In some cases, they were raised as food crops, but they were also grown to supply materials to the construction and chemical industries.

THE SOYBEAN

This is an outstanding example of an ages-old crop that, because of the development of new processes to make its oil and meal more useful, is widely produced today. In the East, where the soybean originated long ago, more than half the crop is used directly for food, and less than a third is pressed for oil. Its high protein and fat content make it a staple in the diet, replacing or supplementing meat for millions of people.

Though first reported grown in America in 1804, the soybean remained a rare garden plant for nearly 100 years. Around the beginning of the 20th century, when three new varieties were introduced from Japan, U.S. farmers began growing it for hay, pasture, and green manure. In the early 1930s a soybean oil processing method that eliminated a disagreeable odour from the finished product was developed. World War II brought an increased demand for edible oil. The food industry began using soybean oil for margarine, shortening, salad oil, mayonnaise, and other food products and continues to be its chief user. Manufacturers of paints, varnishes, and other drying oil products are the most important nonfood users.

Development of the solvent process of extracting soybean oil has greatly increased the yield. A 60-pound bushel of soybeans processed by this method yields 10½ pounds of oil and 45 pounds of meal. Soybean meal and cake are used chiefly for livestock feed in the United States. The high protein content of the meal has made it an attractive source of industrial protein, and, with proper processing, it is an excellent source of protein for humans. By the late 20th century, the centre of soybean production and export had shifted solidly from the eastern to the western hemisphere, with the United States, Brazil, and Argentina leading the industry.

Development of new soybean varieties suited for different parts of the world is possible by means of hybridization. This permits isolating types superior in yielding ability, resistance to lodging (breakage of the plant by wind and rain) and shattering (of the bean), adaptation to suit various requirements for maturity, and resistance to disease. Hybridization, however, has not yet led to spectacular gains in yields.

SORGHUM

Just as the soybean was used for many centuries in Asia before its introduction into the Western world, so sorghum was a major crop in Africa. Sorghum is fifth in importance among the world's cereals, coming after wheat, rice, corn, and barley. It is called by a variety of names including Guinea corn in West Africa, kafir corn in South Africa,

Men and women harvesting sorghum in Burkina Faso. Universal Images Group/Getty Images

durra in Sudan and South Sudan, and mtama in East Africa. In India it is known as jowar, cholam, and great millet, and it is called gaoliang in China. In the United States it is often called milo, while the sweet-stemmed varieties are referred to as sweet sorghum, or sorgo.

Sorghum probably had been domesticated in Ethiopia by 3000 BP. From there, it spread to West and East Africa, and then southward. Traders from Africa to the East carried sorghum as provisions on their dhows. It is likely that sorghum thus reached India, where cultivation began between 1500 and 1000 BP. Other traders carried sorghum to China and the other countries of East Asia. The amber sorghums, or sorgos, useful for forage and syrup, may have moved by sea, while the grain sorghums probably moved overland. The movement to the Mediterranean and Southwest Asia also began through traders.

Sorghum reached the Americas through the slave trade. Guinea corn and chicken corn came from West Africa to America as provisions for the slaves. Other types were introduced into the United States by seedsmen and scientists from about 1870 to 1910. Seed was sometimes sold to farmers as a new, highly productive variety of corn. It was not until the 1930s, after the value of the plant as grain, forage, and silage for livestock feeding had been recognized, that acreage began to increase. Yields rose markedly in the late 1950s, after successful hybridization of the crop. Better yields led in turn to increased acreage.

Chinese ambercane was brought from France to the United States in 1854 and was distributed to farmers. While the cane provided good forage for livestock, promoters of the new crop were most interested in refining sugar from the sorghum molasses, a goal that persisted for many years. While refining technology has been perfected, the present cost of sorghum sugar does not permit it to compete with sugar from other sources.

SORGHUM

The term *sorghum* refers both to a cereal grain plant of the family Gramineae (Poaceae), probably originating in Africa, and to its edible starchy seeds. All types raised chiefly for grain belong to the species *Sorghum vulgare*, which includes varieties of grain sorghums and grass sorghums, grown for hay and fodder, and broomcorn, used in making brooms and brushes. Grain sorghums include durra, milo, shallu, kafir corn, Egyptian corn, great millet, and Indian millet. In India sorghum is known as jowar, cholam, or jonna; in West Africa as Guinea corn; and in China as kaoliang. Sorghum is especially valued in hot and arid regions for its resistance to drought and heat.

The grain is usually ground into a meal that is made into porridge, flatbreads, and cakes. The characteristic strong flavour can be reduced by processing. The grain is also used in making edible oil, starch, dextrose (a sugar), paste, and alcoholic beverages. The stalks are used as fodder and building materials. Sweet sorghums, or sorgos, are grown mainly in the United States and southern Africa for forage and for syrup manufacture. In some countries the sweet stalks are chewed.

Large amounts of sorghum grain are eaten every year by people of many countries. If the world population continues to grow as projected, food is likely to be sorghum's most important use. Most of the sorghum is ground into flour, often at home. Some is consumed as a whole-kernel food. Some of the grain is used for brewing beer, particularly in Africa.

THE SUGAR BEET

The sugar beet as a crop is much newer than either soybeans or sorghum. Although beets had been a source of sweets among ancient Egyptians, Indians, Chinese,

Greeks, and Romans, it was not until 1747 that a German apothecary, Andreas Marggraf, obtained sugar crystals from the beet. Some 50 years later, Franz Karl Achard, son of a French refugee in Prussia and student of Marggraf, improved the Silesian stock beet—probably a mangel-wurzel—as a source of sugar. He erected the first pilot beet-sugar factory at Cunern, Silesia (now Poland), in 1802. Thus began the new use for sugar of a crop traditionally used as animal feed.

When during the Napoleonic Wars continental Europe was cut off from West Indies cane sugar, further experimentation with beet sugar was stimulated. In 1808 a French scientist, Benjamin Delessert, used charcoal in clarification, which insured the technical success of beet sugar. On March 25, 1811, Napoleon issued a decree that set aside 80,000 acres (about 32,375 hectares) of land for the production of beets, established six special sugar-beet schools to which 100 select students were given scholarships, directed construction of 10 new factories, and appropriated substantial bounties to encourage the peasants to grow beets. By 1814, 40 small factories were in operation in France, Belgium, Germany, and Austria. Although the industry declined sharply after Napoleon's defeat, it was soon revived. For the last third of the 19th century, beets replaced cane as the leading source of sugar.

Since World War II, major changes have taken place in sugar-beet production in the United States and, to a lesser extent, in Germany and other countries with a substantial production. These changes may be illustrated by developments in the United States.

In 1931 the California Agricultural Experiment Station and the U.S. Department of Agriculture undertook a cooperative study of the mechanization of sugar-beet growing and harvesting. The goal in harvesting was a combine that would perform all the harvesting operations—lifting from the soil, cutting the tops, and loading—in one trip down the row. By the end of World War II, four different types of harvesters were being manufactured.

The spring and summer operations—planting, blocking (cutting out all plants except for clumps standing 10 to 12 inches [25 to 30 cm] apart), thinning, and weeding—did not yield so easily to mechanization, largely because the beet seed, a multigerm seedball, produced several seedlings, resulting in dense, clumpy, and somewhat irregular stands. In 1941 a machine for segmenting the seedball was developed. The problem was solved in 1948, when a plant with a true single-germ seed was discovered in Oregon. Now precision seed drills could be used, and plants could be first blocked and then cultivated mechanically using a cross-cultivating technique—i.e., cultivating the rows up and down and then across the field. During World War I, 11.2 hours of labour were required to produce a ton of sugar beets; in 1964, 2.7 hours were needed.

NEW TECHNIQUES

As the development of the sugar beet shows, new techniques may bring particular crops into prominence. This discussion, however, is confined to three that, in some forms, are old yet today are transforming agriculture in many parts of the world.

TERRACING

Terracing, which is basically grading steep land, such as hillsides, into a series of level benches, was known in antiquity and was practiced thousands of years ago in such divergent areas as the Philippines, Peru, and Central Africa. Today, terracing is of major importance in Japan, Mexico, and parts of the United States, while many other countries, including Israel, Australia, South Africa, Colombia, and Brazil, are increasing productivity through the inauguration of this and other soil-conserving practices. Colombia and the Brazilian state of São Paulo in particular made use of terracing in a manner that preserved land and improved agricultural production.

IRRIGATION

The usefulness of a full-scale conservation project is seen in the Snowy Mountains Scheme of Australia (1949–74), where three river systems were diverted to convert hundreds of miles of arid but fertile plains to productive land. Intensive soil conservation methods were undertaken wherever the natural vegetation and soil surface had been disturbed. Drainage is controlled by stone and steel drains, grassed waterways, absorption and contour terraces, and settling ponds. Steep slopes are stabilized by woven wickerwork fences, brush matting, and bitumen sprays, followed by revegetation with white clover and willow and poplar trees. Grazing is strictly controlled to prevent silting of the reservoirs and damage to slopes. The two main products of the plan are power for new industries and irrigation water for agriculture, with recreation and a tourist industry as important by-products.

Australia's Snowy Mountains Scheme is a modern successor, so far as irrigation is concerned, to practices that have provided water for crops almost from the beginnings of agriculture. The simplest method of irrigation was to dip water from a well or spring and pour it on the land. Many types of buckets, ropes, and, later, pulleys were employed. The ancient shadoof, which consists of a long pole pivoted from a beam that has a weight at one end to lift a full bucket of water at the other, is still in use. Conduction of water through ditches from streams was practiced widely in Southwest Asia, in Africa, and in the Americas, where ancient canal systems can be seen. A conduit the Romans built 2,000 years ago to provide a water supply to Tunis is still in use.

Sufficient water at the proper time makes possible the full use of technology in farming—including the proper application of fertilizers, suitable crop rotations, and the use of more productive varieties of crops. Expanding irrigation is an absolute necessity to extend crop acreage in significant amounts; it may be the most productive of possible improvements on present cropland. First, there is the possibility of making wider use of irrigation in districts that already have a high rate of output. Second, there is the possibility of irrigating nonproductive land, especially in arid zones. The greatest immediate economic returns might well come from irrigating productive districts, but irrigation of arid zones has a larger long-range appeal. Most of the arid zones, occupying more than one-third of the landmass of the globe, are in the tropics. Generally, they are rich in solar energy, and their soils are rich in nutrients, but they lack water.

Supplemental irrigation in the United States, used primarily to make up for poor distribution of rainfall during the growing season, has increased substantially since the late 1930s. This irrigation is carried on in the humid areas of the United States almost exclusively with sprinkler systems. The water is conveyed in pipes, usually laid on the surface of the field, and the soil acts as a storage reservoir. The water itself is pumped from a stream, lake, well, or reservoir. American farmers first used sprinkler irrigation about 1900, but the development of lightweight aluminum pipe with quick couplers meant that the pipe could be moved easily and quickly from one location to another, resulting in a notable increase in the use of sprinklers after World War II.

India, where irrigation has been practiced since ancient times, illustrates some of the problems. During the late 20th century, more than 20 percent of the country's cultivated area was under irrigation. Two types of dams have been used: large dams, with canals to distribute the water, and small tube, or driven, wells, which are controlled by individual farmers and made by driving a pipe into water or water-bearing sand. Some have been affected by salinity, however, as water containing dissolved salts has been allowed to evaporate in the field. Tube wells have helped in these instances by lowering the water table and by providing sufficient water to flush away the salts. The other major problem has been to persuade Indian farmers to level their lands and build the small canals needed to carry the water over the farms. In Egypt, impounding of the Nile River with the Aswan High Dam has been a great boon to agriculture, but it has also reduced the flow of silt into the Nile Valley and adversely affected fishing in the Mediterranean Sea. In arid areas such as the U.S. Southwest, tapping subterranean water supplies has resulted in a lowered water table and, in some instances, land subsidence.

DRY FARMING

The problem of educating farmers to make effective use of irrigation water is found in many areas. An even greater educational effort is required for dry farming; that is, crop production without irrigation where annual precipitation is less than 20 inches (50 cm).

Dry farming as a system of agriculture was developed in the Great Plains of the United States early in the 20th century. It depended on the efficient storage of the limited moisture in the soil and the selection of crops and growing methods that made best use of this moisture. The system included deep fall plowing, subsurface packing of

A farmer in India digging canals to irrigate his land.
Deshakalyan Chowdhury/AFP/Getty Images

the soil, thorough cultivation both before and after seeding, light seeding, and alternating-summer fallow, with the land tilled during the season of fallow as well as in crop years. In certain latitudes stubble was left in the fields after harvest to trap snow. Though none of the steps were novel, their systematic combination was new. Systematic dry farming has continued, with substantial modifications, in the Great Plains of Canada and the United States, in Brazil, in South Africa, in Australia, and elsewhere. It is under continuing research by the Food and Agriculture Organization of the United Nations.

THE DIRECTION OF CHANGE

While no truly new crop has been developed in modern times, new uses and new methods of cultivation of known plants may be regarded as new crops. For example, subsistence and special-use plants, such as the members of the genus *Atriplex* that are salt-tolerant, have the potential for being developed into new crops. New techniques, too, are the elaboration and systematization of practices from the past.

CHAPTER 8

NEW STRAINS: GENETICS AND THE QUEST FOR PRODUCTIVITY

The use of genetics to develop new strains of plants and animals has brought major changes in agriculture since the 1920s. Genetics as the science dealing with the principles of heredity and variation in plants and animals was established only at the beginning of the 20th century. Its application to practical problems came later.

WORK IN PLANT GENETICS

The modern science of genetics and its application to agriculture has a complicated background, built up from the work of many individuals. Nevertheless, Gregor Mendel is generally credited with its founding. Mendel, a monk in Brünn, Mor. (now Brno, Cz.), purposefully crossed garden peas in his monastery garden. He carefully sorted the progeny of his parent plants according to their characteristics and counted the number that had inherited each quality. He discovered that when the qualities he was studying, including flower colour and shape of seeds, were handed on by the parent plants, they were distributed among the offspring in definite mathematical ratios, from which there was never a significant variation. Definite laws of inheritance were thus established for the first time. Though Mendel reported his discoveries in an obscure Austrian journal in 1866, his work was not followed

Gregor Mendel. Hulton Archive/Getty Images

up for a third of a century. Then in 1900, investigators in the Netherlands, Germany, and Austria, all working on inheritance, independently rediscovered Mendel's paper.

By the time Mendel's work was again brought to light, the science of genetics was in its first stages of development. The word *genetics* comes from *genes*, the name given to the minute quantities of living matter that transmit characteristics from parent to offspring. By 1903 scientists in the United States and Germany had concluded that genes are carried in the chromosomes, nuclear structures visible under the microscope. In 1911 a theory that the genes are arranged in a linear file on the chromosomes and that changes in this conformation are reflected in changes in heredity was announced.

Genes are highly stable. During the processes of sexual reproduction, however, means are present for assortment, segregation, and recombination of genetic factors. Thus, tremendous genetic variability is provided within a species. This variability makes possible the changes that can be brought about within a species to adapt it to specific uses. Occasional mutations (spontaneous changes) of genes also contribute to variability.

Development of new strains of plants and animals did not, of course, await the science of genetics, and some advances were made by empirical methods even after the application of genetic science to agriculture. The U.S. plant breeder Luther Burbank, without any formal knowledge of genetic principles, developed the Burbank potato as early as 1873 and continued his plant-breeding research, which produced numerous new varieties of fruits and vegetables. In some instances, both practical experience and scientific knowledge contributed to major technological achievements. An example is the development of hybrid corn.

MAIZE, OR CORN

Maize originated in the Americas, having been first developed by native peoples in the highlands of Mexico. It was quickly adopted by the European settlers, Spanish, English, and French. The first English settlers found the native peoples of the northern regions growing a hard-kerneled, early-maturing flint variety that kept well, though its yield was low. Indigenous peoples in the south-central area of English settlement grew a soft-kerneled, high-yielding, late-maturing dent corn. There were doubtless many haphazard crosses of the two varieties. In 1812, however, John Lorain, a farmer living near Philipsburg, Pa., consciously mixed the two and demonstrated that certain mixtures would result in a yield much greater than that of the flint, yet with many of the flint's desirable qualities. Other farmers and breeders followed Lorain's example, some aware of his pioneer work, some not. The most widely grown variety of the Corn Belt for many years was Reid's Yellow Dent, which originated from a fortuitous mixture of a dent and a flint variety.

At the same time, other scientists besides Mendel were conducting experiments and developing theories that were to lead directly to hybrid maize. In 1876 Charles Darwin published the results of experiments on cross- and self-fertilization in plants. Carrying out his work in a small greenhouse in his native England, the man who is best known for his theory of evolution found that inbreeding usually reduced plant vigour and that crossbreeding restored it.

Darwin's work was studied by a young American botanist, William James Beal, who probably made the first controlled crosses between varieties of maize for the sole purpose of increasing yields through hybrid vigour. Beal worked successfully without knowledge of the genetic principle involved. In 1908 George Harrison Shull concluded that self-fertilization tended to separate and purify strains while weakening the plants but that vigour could be restored by crossbreeding the inbred strains. Another scientist found that inbreeding could increase the protein content of maize, but with a marked decline in yield. With knowledge of inbreeding and hybridization at hand, scientists had yet to develop a technique whereby hybrid maize with the desired characteristics of the inbred lines and hybrid vigour could be combined in a practical manner. In 1917 Donald F. Jones of the Connecticut Agricultural Experiment Station discovered the answer, the "double cross."

The double cross was the basic technique used in developing modern hybrid maize and has been used by commercial firms since. Jones's invention was to use four inbred lines instead of two in crossing. Simply, inbred lines A and B made one cross, lines C and D another. Then AB and CD were crossed, and a double-cross hybrid, ABCD, was the result. This hybrid became the seed that changed much of American agriculture. Each inbred line was constant both for certain desirable and for certain undesirable traits, but the practical breeder could balance his four or more inbred lines in such a way that the desirable traits outweighed the undesirable. Foundation inbred lines were developed to meet the needs of varying climates, growing seasons, soils, and other factors. The large hybrid seed-corn companies undertook complex applied-research programs, while state experiment stations and the U.S. Department of Agriculture tended to concentrate on basic research.

The first hybrid maize involving inbred lines to be produced commercially was sold by the Connecticut Agricultural Experiment Station in 1921. The second was developed by Henry A. Wallace, a future secretary of agriculture and vice president of the United States. He sold a small quantity in 1924 and, in 1926, organized the first seed company devoted to the commercial production of hybrid maize.

Many Midwestern farmers began growing hybrid maize in the late 1920s and 1930s, but it did not dominate corn production until World War II. In 1933, 1 percent of the total maize acreage was planted with hybrid seed. By 1939 the figure was 15 percent, and in 1946 it rose to 69. The percentage was 96 in 1960. The average per acre yield of maize rose from 23 bushels (2,000 litres per hectare) in 1933, to 83 bushels (7,220 litres per hectare) in 1980, to about 165 bushels (about 14,400 litres per hectare) in 2009.

The techniques used in breeding hybrid maize have been successfully applied to grain sorghum and several other crops. New strains of most major crops are developed through plant introductions, crossbreeding, and selection, however, because hybridization in the sense used with maize and grain sorghums has not been successful with several other crops.

WHEAT

Advances in wheat production during the 20th century included improvements through the introduction of new varieties and strains; careful selection by farmers and seedsmen, as well as by scientists; and crossbreeding to combine desirable characteristics. The adaptability of wheat enables it to be grown in almost every country of the world. In most of the developed countries producing wheat, endeavours of both government and wheat growers have been directed toward scientific wheat breeding.

The development of the world-famous Marquis wheat in Canada, released to farmers in 1900, came about through sustained scientific effort. Sir Charles Saunders, its discoverer, followed five principles of plant breeding: (1) the use of plant introductions; (2) a planned cross-breeding program; (3) the rigid selection of material; (4) evaluation of all characteristics in replicated trials; and (5) testing varieties for local use. Marquis was the result of crossing a wheat long grown in Canada with a variety introduced from India. For 50 years, Marquis and varieties crossbred from Marquis dominated hard red spring wheat growing in the high plains of Canada and the United States and were used in other parts of the world.

In the late 1940s a short-stemmed wheat was introduced from Japan into a more favourable wheat-growing region of the U.S. Pacific Northwest. The potential advantage of the short, heavy-stemmed plant was that it could carry a heavy head of grain, generated by the use of fertilizer, without falling over or "lodging" (being knocked down). Early work with the variety was unsuccessful; it was not adaptable directly into U.S. fields. Finally, by crossing the Japanese wheat with acceptable varieties in the Palouse Valley in Washington, there resulted the first true semidwarf wheat in the United States to be commercially grown under irrigation and heavy applications of fertilizer. This first variety, Gaines, was introduced in 1962, followed by Nugaines in 1966. The varieties grown in the United States have produced 100 bushels per acre (8,700 litres per hectare), and world records of more than 200 bushels per acre have been established.

The Rockefeller Foundation in 1943 entered into a cooperative agricultural research program with the government of Mexico, where wheat yields were well below the world average. By 1956 per acre yield had doubled, mainly because of newly developed varieties sown in the fall instead of spring and the use of fertilizers and irrigation. The short-stemmed varieties developed in the Pacific Northwest from the Japanese strains were then crossed with various Mexican and Colombian wheats. By 1965 the new Mexican wheats were established, and they gained an international reputation.

RICE

The success of the wheat program led the Rockefeller and Ford foundations in 1962 to establish the International Rice Research Institute at Los Baños in the Philippines. A research team assembled some 10,000 strains of rice from all parts of the world and began outbreeding. Success came early with the combination of a tall, vigorous variety from Indonesia and a dwarf rice from Taiwan. The strain IR-8 proved capable of doubling the yield obtained from most local rices in Asia.

THE GREEN REVOLUTION

The introduction into developing countries of new strains of wheat and rice was a major aspect of what became known as the Green Revolution. Given adequate water and ample amounts of the required chemical fertilizers and pesticides, these varieties have resulted in significantly higher yields. Poorer farmers, however, often have not been able to provide the required growing conditions and therefore have obtained even lower yields with "improved" grains than they had gotten with the older strains that were better adapted to local conditions and that had some resistance to pests and diseases. Where chemicals are used, concern has been voiced about their cost—since they generally must be imported—and about their potentially harmful effects on the environment.

GENETIC ENGINEERING

The application of genetics to agriculture since World War II has resulted in substantial increases in the production of many crops. This has been most notable in hybrid strains of maize and grain sorghum. At the same time, crossbreeding has resulted in much more productive strains of wheat and rice. Called artificial selection, or selective breeding, these techniques have become aspects of a larger and somewhat controversial field called genetic engineering. Of particular interest to plant breeders has been the development of techniques for deliberately altering the functions of genes by manipulating the

One variety of genetically modified soybean growing in Brazil. Bloomberg/Getty Images

recombination of DNA (the organic chemical that carries the genetic information that governs inherited traits). This has made it possible for researchers to concentrate on creating plants that possess attributes—such as the ability to use free nitrogen or to resist diseases—that they did not have naturally. During the second half of the 20th century, genetically modified (GM) crops became widespread in the United States: by 1999, for example, almost 50 percent of the corn, cotton, and soybeans planted there were GM. By 2010 nearly one-tenth of the world's farmland was covered with GM crops.

GENETIC IMPROVEMENT IN LIVESTOCK

The goal of animal breeders in the 20th century was to develop types of animals that would meet market demands, be productive under adverse climatic conditions, and be efficient in converting feed to animal products. At the same time, producers increased meat production by improved range management, better feeding practices, and the eradication of diseases and harmful insects. The world production of meat has been increasing steadily since World War II.

While the number of livestock in relation to the human population is not significantly lower in less developed than in more developed regions, there is much lower productivity per animal and thus a much lower percentage of livestock products in diets. Less scientific breeding practices usually prevail in the less developed regions, while great care is given to animal breeding in the more developed regions of North America, Europe, Australia, and New Zealand.

The advances made in developing new, highly productive strains of crops through the application of genetics have not been matched by similar advances in livestock. Except for broiler chickens in the United States, little progress has been made in improving the efficiency with which animals convert feed to animal products. Research on the breeding and nutrition of poultry, for example, makes it possible to produce chickens for market in about 30 percent less time than it took before the research findings were applied.

HOGS

Advances in animal breeding have been made by careful selection and crossbreeding. These techniques are not new. The major breeds of English cattle, for example, were developed in the 18th and early 19th centuries by selection and crossbreeding. The Poland China and Duroc Jersey breeds of swine were developed in the United States in the latter part of the 19th century by the same means.

The hogs developed in the United States in the latter part of the 19th and first part of the 20th century were heavy, fat-producing animals that met the demands for lard. During the 1920s lard became less important as a source of fat because of increasing use of cheaper vegetable oils. Meat-packers then sought hogs yielding more lean meat and less fat, even though market prices moved rather slowly toward making their production profitable.

At the same time, Danish, Polish, and other European breeders were crossbreeding swine to obtain lean meat and vigorous animals. An outstanding new breed was the Danish Landrace, which in the 1930s was crossed with several older American breeds, eventually giving rise to several new, mildly inbred lines. These lines produced more lean meat and less fat, as well as larger litters and bigger pigs.

SHEEP

Similar crossbreeding, followed by intermating and selection with the crossbreeds, brought major changes in the sheep industries of New Zealand and the United States. The goal in New Zealand was to produce more acceptable meat animals, while that in the United States was to produce animals suited to Western range conditions and acceptable both for wool and mutton.

During the late 19th century, several New Zealand sheep breeders began crossing Lincoln and Leicester rams with Merino ewes. Early in the 20th century, the Corriedale had become established as a breed, carrying approximately 50 percent Australian Merino, with Leicester and Lincoln blood making up the remainder. The Corriedale was successfully introduced into the United States in 1914. Since World War II, a more uniform lamb carcass has been developed in New Zealand by crossing Southdown rams with Romney ewes.

With different objectives in view, breeders in the United States in 1912 made initial crosses between the long-wool mutton breed, the Lincoln, and fine-wool Rambouillets. Subsequent intermating and selection within the crossbreds led to a new breed, the Columbia. Both the Columbia and the Targhee, another breed developed in the same way as the Columbia, have been widely used. They are suited to the Western ranges, and they serve reasonably well both as wool and meat animals.

BEEF CATTLE

Changes in beef cattle, particularly the establishment of new breeds, have resulted from selective linebreeding and from crossbreeding. The Polled Shorthorn and the Polled Hereford breeds were established by locating and

Two Beefmaster cattle being moved during a 2004 convention for Beefmaster breeders in Texas. © AP Images

breeding the few naturally hornless animals to be found among the horned herds of Shorthorns and Herefords, first established as distinctive breeds in England. It is of particular note that the originator of the Polled Herefords made an effort to locate naturally hornless Herefords and begin linebreeding with them after he had studied Darwin's work on mutations and variations and how they could be made permanent by systematic mating.

Three new breeds originating in the United States were developed for parts of the South where the standard breeds lacked resistance to heat and insects and did not thrive on the native grasses. The first of these breeds, the Santa Gertrudis, was developed on the King Ranch in Texas by crossbreeding Shorthorns and Brahmans, a heat- and insect-resistant breed from India. The Santa Gertrudis cattle carry approximately five-eighths Shorthorn blood and three-eighths Brahman. They are heavy beef cattle and thrive in hot climates and were exported to South and Central America in order to upgrade the native cattle.

The Brangus breed was developed in the 1930s and 1940s by crossing Brahman and Angus cattle. The breed has been standardized with three-eighths Brahman and five-eighths Angus breeding. The Brangus generally have the hardiness of the Brahman for Southern conditions but the improved carcass qualities of the Angus.

The Beefmaster was developed in Texas and Colorado by crossbreeding and careful selection, with the cattle carrying about one-half Brahman blood and about one-fourth each of Hereford and Shorthorn breeding. Emphasis was given to careful selection, major points being disposition, fertility, weight, conformation, hardiness, and milk production.

ARTIFICIAL BREEDING

An increase in milk production per cow in the 20th century was brought about through better nutrition and artificial breeding. Artificial breeding permits the use of proved sires, developed through successive crosses of animals of proved merit. An Italian scientist experimented successfully with artificial insemination in 1780, but its practical usefulness was not demonstrated until the 20th century. The Soviet biologist Ilya Ivanov established the Central Experimental Breeding Station in Moscow in 1919 to continue work that he had begun some 20 years earlier. As early as 1936, more than six million cattle and sheep were artificially inseminated in the Soviet Union.

After the Soviets reported their successes, scientists in many countries experimented with artificial breeding. Denmark began with dairy cattle in the 1930s. The first group in the United States began work in 1938. Statistics show that the milk and butterfat production of proved sires' daughters, resulting from artificial breeding, is higher than that of other improved dairy cattle. Furthermore, a single sire can be used to inseminate 2,000 cows a year, as compared with 30 to 50 in natural breeding.

In summary, crossbreeding and careful selection, combined with such techniques as artificial insemination, better feeding, and control of diseases and pests, made substantial contributions to livestock production in the 20th century that have continued to pay benefits today.

CHAPTER 9
ELECTRICITY, PEST CONTROL, AND THE REGULATION OF AGRICULTURE

The impact of electric power on modern agriculture has been at least as significant as that of either steam or gasoline, because electricity in its nature is far more versatile than the earlier power sources. Ultimately, electrification of farms has allowed agricultural productivity to increase tremendously. Also important has been the development of means by which to eradicate harmful bugs and plant disease from fields. The development of large-scale agriculture also generated trade imbalances and other economic issues that necessitated regulation of agricultural production and exchange on both national and international levels.

ELECTRIFICATION OF FARMS

There had long been scientific interest on the effects of electricity on plant growth, especially after the development of electric lamps. It was the development of the electric motor, however, that really gained the interest of the farming community. Some authorities saw its value to farmers as early as 1870.

ELECTRICAL COOPERATIVES

Despite the obvious advantages of the other, more available power sources, progressive farmers in a number of countries were determined to exploit the possibilities of electricity on their farms. To get electricity, farmers formed cooperatives that either bought bulk power from existing facilities or built their own generating stations.

It is believed that the first such cooperatives were formed in Japan in 1900, followed by similar organizations in Germany in 1901. Multiplying at a considerable rate, these farmer cooperatives not only initiated rural electrification as such but provided the basis for its future development.

A threshing machine with an electric engine, c. 1913. Boyer/ Roger Viollet/Getty Images

From these small beginnings the progress of rural electrification, though necessarily slow, steadily gained impetus until, in the 1920s, public opinion eventually compelled governments to consider the development of rural electrification on a national basis. Today in the more developed countries virtually all rural premises— domestic, commercial, industrial, and farms—have an adequate supply of electricity.

Early applications of electricity were of necessity restricted to power and some lighting, although the full value of lighting was not completely realized for years. Electric motors were used to drive barn machinery, chaffcutters and root cutters, cattle cake and grain crushers, and water pumps. Electricity's ease of operation and low maintenance showed savings in time and labour. It was not long before the electric motor began to replace the mobile steam engine on threshing, winnowing, and other crop-processing equipment outside the barn.

In the fields, a number of electrically driven, rope-haulage plowing installations, some of them quite large, came into use in several European countries. These systems, however, did not stand the test of time or competition from the mobile internal-combustion-driven tractor.

Applications of electricity in agriculture did not increase greatly until the 1920s, when economic pressures and the increasing drift of labour from the land brought about a change in the whole structure of agriculture. This change, based on new techniques of intensive crop production resulting from the development of a wide range of mechanical, electrical, and electromechanical equipment, was the start of the evolution of agriculture from a labour-intensive industry to the present capital-intensive industry, and in this electricity played a major part.

MODERN APPLICATIONS

Modern applications of electricity in farming range from the comparatively simple to some as complex as those in the manufacturing industries. They include conditioning and storage of grain and grass; preparation and rationing of animal feed; and provision of a controlled environment in stock-rearing houses for intensive pig and poultry rearing and in greenhouses for horticultural crops. Electricity plays an equally important part in the dairy farm for feed rationing, milking, and milk cooling; all these applications are automatically controlled, with computers playing a crucial role in farm management and in the control of automated equipment.

The engineer and farmer have combined to develop electrically powered equipment for crop conservation and storage to help overcome weather hazards at harvest time and to reduce labour requirements to a minimum. Grain can now be harvested in a matter of days instead of months and dried to required moisture content for prolonged storage by means of electrically driven fans and, in many installations, gas or electrical heaters. Wilted grass, cut at the stage of maximum feeding value, can be turned into high-quality hay in the barn by means of forced ventilation and with very little risk of spoilage loss from inclement weather.

Conditioning and storage of such root crops as potatoes, onions, carrots, and beets, in especially designed stores with forced ventilation and temperature control, and of fruit in refrigerated stores are all electrically based techniques that minimize waste and maintain top quality over longer periods than was possible with traditional methods of storage.

The two most significant changes in the pattern of agricultural development that have been enabled by electrification are (1) the degree to which specialization has been adopted and (2) the increased scale of farm enterprises. These changes began in the years after World War II but continue to strongly influence agriculture today. Large numbers of beef cattle are raised in enclosures and fed carefully balanced rations by automatic equipment. Pigs by the thousands and poultry by the tens of thousands are housed in special buildings with controlled environments and are fed automatically with complex rations. Dairy herds of 1,000 cows are machine-milked in milking parlours, and the cows are then individually identified and fed appropriate rations by complex electronic equipment. The milk passes directly from the cow into refrigerated bulk milk tanks and is ready for immediate shipment. The increasing scale of agriculture in the United States in particular was such that, at the turn of the 21st century, critics deployed the derisive term *factory farming* to describe livestock operations in which large populations of animals were raised in crowded environments and treated with antibiotics to encourage quick growth.

PEST AND DISEASE CONTROL IN CROPS

Wherever agriculture has been practiced, pests have attacked, destroying part or even all of the crop. The period from the mid-19th to the early 20th century was characterized by increasing awareness of the possibilities of avoiding losses from pests, by the rise of firms specializing in pesticide manufacture, and by development of better application machinery.

BEGINNINGS OF PEST CONTROL

In modern usage, the term *pest* includes animals (mostly insects), fungi, plants, bacteria, and viruses. Human efforts to control pests have a long history. Even in Neolithic times (about 7000 BP), farmers practiced a crude form of biological pest control involving the more or less unconscious selection of seed from resistant plants. Severe locust attacks in the Nile Valley during the 13th century BP are dramatically described in the Bible, and, in his *Natural History*, the Roman author Pliny the Elder describes picking insects from plants by hand and spraying. The scientific study of pests was not undertaken until the 17th and 18th centuries. The first successful large-scale conquest of a pest by chemical means was the control of the vine powdery mildew (*Unciluna necator*) in Europe in the 1840s. The disease, brought from the Americas, was controlled first by spraying with lime sulfur and, subsequently, by sulfur dusting.

Another serious epidemic was the potato blight that caused famine in Ireland in 1845 and some subsequent years and severe losses in many other parts of Europe and the United States. Insects and fungi from Europe became serious pests in the United States, too. Among these were the European corn borer, the gypsy moth, and the chestnut blight, which practically annihilated that tree.

The first book to deal with pests in a scientific way was John Curtis's *Farm Insects*, published in 1860. Though farmers were well aware that insects caused losses, Curtis was the first writer to call attention to their significant economic impact. The successful battle for control of the Colorado potato beetle (*Leptinotarsa decemlineata*) of the western United States also occurred in the 19th century. When miners and pioneers brought the potato into the Colorado region, the beetle fell upon this crop and became a severe pest, spreading steadily eastward and devastating crops, until it reached the Atlantic. It crossed the ocean and eventually established itself in Europe. But an American entomologist in 1877 found a practical control method consisting of spraying with water-insoluble chemicals such as London Purple, paris green, and calcium and lead arsenates.

Other pesticides that were developed soon thereafter included nicotine, pyrethrum, derris, quassia, and tar oils, first used, albeit unsuccessfully, in 1870 against the winter eggs of the *Phylloxera* plant louse. The Bordeaux mixture fungicide (copper sulfate and lime), discovered accidentally in 1882, was used successfully against vine downy mildew; this compound is still employed to combat it and potato blight. Since many insecticides available in the 19th century were comparatively weak, other pest-control methods were used as well. A species of ladybird

Ladybird beetles feeding on cottony-cushion scale insects that often threaten the citrus industry. Jeffrey W. Lotz, Florida Department of Agriculture and Consumer Services, Bugwood. org

beetle, *Rodolia cardinalis*, was imported from Australia to California, where it controlled the cottony-cushion scale then threatening to destroy the citrus industry. A moth introduced into Australia destroyed the prickly pear, which had made millions of acres of pasture useless for grazing. In the 1880s the European grapevine was saved from destruction by grape phylloxera through the simple expedient of grafting it onto certain resistant American rootstocks.

PESTICIDES AS A PANACEA: 1942–62

In 1942 the Swiss chemist Paul Hermann Müller discovered the insecticidal properties of a synthetic chlorinated organic chemical, dichlorodiphenyltrichloroethane, which was first synthesized in 1874 and subsequently became known as DDT. Müller received the Nobel Prize for Physiology or Medicine in 1948 for his discovery. DDT was far more persistent and effective than any previously known insecticide. Originally a mothproofing agent for clothes, it soon found use among the armies of World War II for killing body lice and fleas. It also stopped a typhus epidemic threatening Naples. Müller's work led to discovery of other chlorinated insecticides, including aldrin, introduced in 1948; chlordane (1945); dieldrin (1948); endrin (1951); heptachlor (1948); methoxychlor (1945); and Toxaphene (1948).

Research on poison gas in Germany during World War II led to the discovery of another group of yet more powerful insecticides and acaricides (killers of ticks and mites)—the organophosphorus compounds, some of which had systemic properties; that is, the plant absorbed them without harm and became itself toxic to insects. The first systemic was octamethylpyrophosphoramide, trade named Schradan. Other organophosphorus insecticides of enormous power were also made, the most common being diethyl-*p*-nitrophenyl monothiophosphate, named parathion. Though low in cost, these compounds were toxic to humans and other warm-blooded animals. The products can poison by absorption through the skin, as well as through the mouth or lungs, thus, spray operators must wear respirators and special clothing. Systemic insecticides need not be carefully sprayed, however; the compound may be absorbed by watering the plant.

Though the advances made in the fungicide field in the first half of the 20th century were not as spectacular as those made with insecticides and herbicides, certain dithiocarbamates, methylthiuram disulfides, and thaladimides were found to have special uses. It began to seem that almost any pest, disease, or weed problem could be mastered by suitable chemical treatment. Farmers foresaw a pest-free millennium. Crop losses were cut sharply; locust attack was reduced to a manageable problem; and the new chemicals, by killing carriers of human disease, saved the lives of millions of people.

Problems appeared in the early 1950s. In cotton crops standard doses of DDT, parathion, and similar pesticides were found ineffective and had to be doubled or tripled. Resistant races of insects had developed. In addition, the powerful insecticides often destroyed natural predators and helpful parasites along with harmful insects. Insects and mites can reproduce at such a rapid rate that often when natural predators were destroyed by a pesticide treatment, a few pest survivors from the treatment, unchecked in breeding, soon produced worse outbreaks of pests than there had been before the treatment; sometimes the result was a population explosion to pest status of previously harmless insects.

At about the same time, concern also began to be expressed about the presence of pesticide residues in food, humans, and wildlife. It was found that many birds and wild mammals retained considerable quantities of DDT in their bodies, accumulated along their natural food chains. The disquiet caused by this discovery was epitomized in 1962 by the publication in the United States of a book entitled *Silent Spring*, whose author, Rachel Carson, attacked the indiscriminate use of pesticides, drew attention to various abuses, and stimulated a reappraisal of pest control. Thus began a new "integrated" approach, which was in effect a return to the use of all methods of control in place of a reliance on chemicals alone.

INTEGRATED CONTROL

Some research into biological methods was undertaken by governments, and in many countries plant breeders began to develop and patent new pest-resistant plant varieties.

One method of biological control involved the breeding and release of males sterilized by means of gamma rays. Though sexually potent, such insects have inactive sperm. Released among the wild population, they mate with the females, who either lay sterile eggs or none at all. The method was used with considerable success against the screwworm, a pest of cattle, in Texas. A second method of biological control employed lethal genes. It is sometimes possible to introduce a lethal or weakening gene into a pest population, leading to the breeding of intersex (effectively neuter) moths or a predominance of males. Various studies have also been made on the chemical identification of substances attracting pests to the opposite sex or to food. With such substances traps can be devised that attract only a specific pest species. Finally, certain chemicals have been fed to insects to sterilize them. Used in connection with a food lure, these can lead to the elimination of a pest from an area. Chemicals tested so far, however, have been considered too dangerous to humans and other mammals for any general use.

Some countries (notably the United States, Sweden, and the United Kingdom) have partly or wholly banned the use of DDT because of its persistence and accumulation in human body fat and its effect on wildlife. New pesticides of lesser human toxicity have been found, one of the most used being mercaptosuccinate, trade named Malathion. A more recent important discovery was the systemic fungicide, absorbed by the plant and transmitted throughout it, making it resistant to certain diseases.

The majority of pesticides are sprayed on crops as solutions or suspensions in water. Spraying machinery has developed from the small hand syringes and "garden engines" of the 18th century to the very powerful "auto-blast machines" of the 1950s that were capable of applying up to some 400 gallons per acre (4,000 litres per hectare). Though spraying suspended or dissolved pesticide was effective, it involved moving a great quantity of inert material for only a relatively small amount of active ingredient. Low-volume spraying was invented about 1950, particularly for the application of herbicides, in which 10 or 20 gallons of water, transformed into fine drops, would carry the pesticide. Ultralow-volume spraying was also introduced; four ounces (about 110 grams) of the active ingredient itself (usually Malathion) are applied to an acre from aircraft. The spray as applied is invisible to the naked eye.

ECONOMICS, POLITICS, AND AGRICULTURE

Agriculture has always been influenced by the actions of governments around the world. Never has this been more evident than during the first half of the 20th century, when two major wars profoundly disrupted food production. In response to the tumultuous economic climate,

European countries implemented tariffs and other measures to protect local agriculture. Such initiatives had global ramifications, and by the mid-20th century various international organizations had been established to monitor and promote agricultural development and the well-being of rural societies. A number of these organizations remain active today.

Western Europe, as the 20th century opened, was recovering from an economic depression during which most of the countries had turned to protecting agriculture through tariffs, with the major exceptions being Great Britain, Denmark, and the Netherlands. In the first decade of the century there was an increasing demand for agricultural products, which was a result of industrialization and population growth, but World War I produced devastating losses in land fertility, livestock, and capital. The resulting shortage of food supplies did, however, benefit farmers for a time, until expanded production and a generalized recovery across Europe depressed prices in the 1920s. Agricultural tariffs, generally suspended during the war, were gradually reintroduced.

The Great Depression of the 1930s brought a new wave of protectionism, leading some industrial countries to look toward self-sufficiency in food supplies. In countries such as France, Germany, and Italy, where agriculture was already protected, the tariff structure was reinforced by new and more drastic measures, while countries such as Britain, Denmark, the Netherlands, and Belgium abandoned free trade and began to support their farmers in a variety of ways. The United States first raised tariffs and then undertook to maintain the prices of farm products. Major exporters of farm products, such as Argentina, Brazil, Australia, Canada, and New Zealand, tried a number of plans to maintain prices.

One of the most effective of the nontariff measures was the "milling ratio" for wheat or, less often, rye, under which millers were legally obliged to use a certain minimum percentage of domestically produced grain in their grist. Although used in only a few European countries in the 1920s, this device became customary in Europe and also in some non-European countries from 1930 up to World War II. Import quotas, adopted on a large scale across Europe and elsewhere, also became a major protective device during the 1930s. The most radical measures, however, were undertaken in Germany under Adolf Hitler, where the Nazi government, seeking self-sufficiency in food, fixed farm prices at relatively high levels and maintained complete control over imports.

Some exporting countries adopted extreme measures during the Depression in an attempt to maintain prices for their commodities. Brazil burned surplus coffee stocks, destroying more than eight billion pounds of coffee over 10 years beginning in 1931. An Inter-American Coffee Agreement, signed in 1940, assigned export quotas to producer countries for shipment to the United States and other consuming countries and was effective during World War II. Other commodity agreements met with very limited success.

Just as World War I significantly lowered food production in Europe, so too did World War II. Agricultural production declined in most of the European countries, shipping became difficult, and trade channels shifted. In contrast, agriculture in the United States, undisturbed by military action and with assurance of full demand and relatively high prices, increased productivity. The United States, Great Britain, and Canada cooperated in a combined food board to allocate available supplies. The United Nations Relief and Rehabilitation Administration (UNRRA) was organized in 1943 to administer postwar relief, while the Food and Agriculture Organization (FAO) of the United Nations was established in 1945 to provide education and technical assistance for agricultural development throughout the world.

Through postwar assistance given primarily by the United States and the United Nations, recovery in Europe was rapid. Western Europe was greatly helped from 1948 on by U.S. aid under the Marshall Plan, administered through the Organisation for European Economic Co-operation (OEEC). In September 1961, this organization was replaced by the Organisation for Economic Co-operation and Development (OECD), which subsequently pursued agricultural programs that dealt, for example, with economic policies, standardization, and development. The eventual expansion of the OECD's membership to a number of non-European countries underscores the manner in

The headquarters of the Food and Agriculture Organization of the United Nations in Rome, Italy. Bloomberg/Getty Images

FOOD AND AGRICULTURE ORGANIZATION (FAO)

The oldest permanent specialized agency of the United Nations is the Food and Agriculture Organization (FAO), established in October 1945 with the objective of eliminating hunger and improving nutrition and standards of living by increasing agricultural productivity. The FAO coordinates the efforts of governments and technical agencies in programs for developing agriculture, forestry, fisheries, and land and water resources. It also carries out research; provides technical assistance on projects in individual countries; operates educational programs through seminars and training centres; maintains information and support services, including keeping statistics on world production, trade, and consumption of agricultural commodities; and publishes a number of periodicals, yearbooks, and research bulletins.

Headquartered in Rome, Italy, the FAO maintains offices throughout the world. The organization, which has more than 190 members, is governed by the biennial FAO conference, in which each member country, as well as the European Union, is represented. The conference elects a 49-member Council, which serves as its executive organ. In the late 20th century the FAO gradually became more decentralized, with about half its personnel working in field offices.

During the 1960s the FAO concentrated on programs for the development of high-yield strains of grain, the elimination of protein deficiencies, the provision of rural employment, and the promotion of agricultural exports. In 1969 the organization published An Indicative World Plan for Agricultural Development, which analyzed the main problems in world agriculture and suggested strategies for solving them. The 1974 World Food Conference, held in Rome during a period of food shortages in the southern Sahara, prompted the FAO to promote programs relating to world food security, including helping small farmers implement low-cost projects to enhance productivity. Today FAO programs for sustainable agriculture and rural development emphasize strategies that are economically feasible, environmentally sound, and technologically accessible to the host country.

which, in the decades after World War II, the story of agriculture's relationship to politics and economics became a truly global one.

Today, most developed countries offer some type of protection to their farmers—price supports, import quotas, and plans for handling surplus production. Notable examples are the agricultural programs run by the U.S. Department of Agriculture and by the European Union. On the other hand, many of the developing countries have had food deficits, with little in the way of exportable goods to pay for food imports. Several national and international organizations have been established in an effort to deal with the problems of the developing countries, and direct assistance has also been provided by the governments of developed countries.

Individual farmers in the countries where commercial agriculture is important have been forced to make changes to meet problems caused by world surpluses and resultant low world prices for farm products. Thus, in many countries, farmers increased productivity through adopting advanced technology. This has permitted each worker, generally speaking, to farm larger areas and has thus reduced the number of farmers. In some countries, commercialization has led to farming by large-scale corporations, and the world tendency is increasingly toward larger farms. The farm operated by a single family, however, is still the dominant unit of production in much of the developing world.

CONCLUSION

From the earliest times, humankind has shown a remarkable capacity to harness nature to its own advantage. Perhaps nowhere has this been more evident than in the realm of agriculture. Domestication began at least 11,000 years ago, and as a result, seeds got bigger, plants fruited faster (and more furiously), and crops became more resistant to quirks of climate and other environmental adversity. Animals were raised to provide service, dairy products, meat, and manure. In the process, they, too, developed various characteristics that made them better suited for their ultimate agricultural purpose.

As people became more skilled in their agricultural pursuits, they reduced their hunting and gathering activities and adopted more settled lifestyles. East Asian people domesticated rice at least 8,500 years ago, and over the next two millennia they established rice-based agricultural communities across the region. Similarly, agricultural villages emerged nearly 7,000 years ago in the Tigris and Euphrates river basins of Southwest Asia and along the Nile River in Egypt. The ancient Egyptians were especially adept at developing irrigation and other forms of water management to increase the volume and quality of crop yields. Some 5,000 years ago, booming urban centres based on farm products such as barley, wheat, sheep, and cattle flourished on the Indian subcontinent. Roughly a thousand years later, agricultural settlements appeared in the Americas. Like the Egyptians, Mesoamericans developed elaborate systems of water management, sculpting spectacular terraces on mountain slopes to store and to regulate the flow of water.

Agriculture was well established in Europe by the time of the Romans. From the third century BCE through the

Middle Ages, European farmers made notable advances not only in the development of agricultural implements but also in land management. Improvements in plows and hand tools facilitated the farming process, while reclamation of land from the forest as well as from the sea increased the availability of areas for cultivation. New crops, such as sugarcane and various subtropical fruits, were also introduced. From the 13th through the 15th century, however, European agriculture suffered serious setbacks owing to famine, disease, and warfare.

When Europe emerged from its recession, major strides were made in the systemization of farming. Most significant was the establishment of the Norfolk four-course system of crop rotation. Based on a four-year cycle, this system consistently yielded food for human consumption, fodder for animals, range lands for livestock, and manure for fertilization. Also important was the move toward the consolidation and enclosure of fields with a fence or other barrier. Such demarcation of lands allowed farmers to manage their agricultural activities more effectively.

The 19th and 20th centuries brought many technological advances to agriculture as an industry. In the 19th century, complex steam-powered machinery was created to facilitate farm preparation, planting, and harvesting. It was not long, however, before steam-powered devices were replaced in the 20th century by combustion engines, which powered tractors as well as an array of new machines dedicated to the harvest of particular crops (e.g., small grains, corn, cotton). Combustion engines also propelled automobiles, trucks, and airplanes, which became indispensable to the distribution of agricultural products. Electrification of farms also augmented productivity by allowing many tasks—such as feeding and milking—to be performed automatically.

Agricultural achievements since the 20th century have by no means been limited to increasingly sophisticated gadgetry. Indeed, monumental discoveries in genetics have enabled scientists to engineer plants and animals that are ideally suited to various environmental and economic settings. Human-made fertilizers, moreover, have significantly increased crop yield, while inorganic and organic pesticides have helped prevent loss of crops to disease and insect infestation. In the wake of such accomplishments, farming has exploded as a commercial enterprise. Consequently, local and national governments have found it necessary to regulate agricultural activities to maintain a well-nourished population and a healthy economy. In 1945 the Food and Agriculture Organization (FAO) of the United Nations was established to monitor and assist agricultural planning on an international scale, and the active role it continues to play today in rural development underscores the worldwide importance of agriculture in the 21st century.

GLOSSARY

alluvium Soil material (as clay, silt, sand, or gravel) deposited by running water, especially rivers and streams.

chinampa A Mexican artificial meadow or garden reclaimed from a lake or pond by piling soil dredged from the bottom onto a mat of twigs and planting thereon.

crop-and-fallow system Also known as the two-field system, a system of crop rotation in which the land is divided into two parts alternately left fallow.

fallow Left untilled or unsown after plowing.

friable Easily crumbled or pulverized.

harrow A cultivating tool that has spikes, teeth, or disks and is used for breaking up and smoothing the soil.

husbandry The cultivation or production of plants or animals.

loess Fine, usually yellowish brown soil that is found in North America, Europe, and Asia and is deposited chiefly by the wind.

mattock A picklike tool for digging that consists of a long wooden handle attached to a steel head, which comes to a point at one end and to a cutting edge at the other.

métayer One who cultivates land for a share of its yield, usually receiving stock, tools, and seed from the landlord.

mutation An inherited physical or chemical change in genetic material.

natural selection A natural process enabling the ultimate survival and reproduction of those organisms that are best adapted to their environment.

Norfolk four-course system Method of agricultural organization established in Norfolk county, Eng., and in several other counties before the end of the 17th century; it was characterized by an emphasis on fodder crops and by the absence of a fallow year, which had characterized earlier methods.

one-crop system An agricultural system marked by the cultivation of only one type of crop on the same land over many seasons.

open-field system A system of agriculture typical of medieval Europe, whereby lands were divided into strips, with different farmers cultivating multiple strips scattered across a number of fields; cultivation was usually based on a 3-year rotation, with some lands reserved for common grazing.

phenotype The visible characteristics of a plant or animal that result from the interaction of its total genetic constitution with the environment.

phytolith A microscopic silica particle that is formed by a plant and that is highly resistant to decomposition.

polder A tract of low land (as in the Netherlands) reclaimed from a body of water (as the sea).

rhizome A fleshy, rootlike, and usually horizontal underground plant stem that produces shoots above and roots below.

sexual dimorphism The differences in appearance between males and females of the same species, as in colour, shape, size, and structure, that are caused by the inheritance of one or the other sexual pattern in the genetic material.

swidden A piece of land that has been cleared by cutting back and burning off vegetative cover to form a temporary agricultural plot.

thresh To separate seed from a harvested plant, especially by using a machine or tool.

transhumance Seasonal herding of livestock (as sheep) between mountain and lowland pastures.

winnow To blow air through threshed grain in order to remove the separated husks.

BIBLIOGRAPHY

B.D. Smith, *The Emergence of Agriculture* (1995), is an integrated overview of research methods, theoretical considerations, and archaeological sites pertinent to the development of agriculture. M. Woods and M.B. Woods, *Ancient Agriculture: From Foraging to Farming* (2000), discusses agricultural technology in various cultures from the Stone Age to 476 CE, including China, Egypt, Mesoamerica, and Greece. J. Desmond Clark and Steven A. Brandt (eds.), *From Hunters to Farmers: The Causes and Consequences of Food Production in Africa* (1984), analyzes economic changes in prehistoric society; T.D. Price, *Europe's First Farmers* (2000), gives an account of the development of farming in Europe. D.R. Piperno and D.M. Pearsall, *The Origins of Agriculture in the Lowland Neotropics* (1998), is the first assessment of the history and significance of tropical lowland agriculture in the Americas. Two excellent volumes that consider the designation of a fourth agricultural regime in North America are Douglas Deur and Nancy J. Turner (eds.), *Keeping it Living: Traditions of Plant Use and Cultivation on the Northwest Coast of North America* (2005); and Kat Anderson, *Tending the Wild: Native American Knowledge and the Management of California's Natural Resources* (2005). R. Douglas Hurt, *American Agriculture: A Brief History*, rev. ed. (2002), provides a broad overview from prehistoric times through the 20th century.

Peter S. Bellwood, *First Farmers: The Origins of Agricultural Societies* (2005), assesses the beginning and diffusion of agriculture around the world. C. Wesley

Cowan, Patty Jo Watson, and Nancy L. Benco, *The Origins of Agriculture: An International Perspective*, new ed. (2006), is a region-by-region review of current data, particularly plant and animal remains from archaeological sites. N.I. Vavilov, *The Origin, Variation, Immunity, and Breeding of Cultivated Plants* (1951), presents selected writings of one of the world's outstanding contributors to the theory of genetics, plant breeding, and study of plant variation, systematics, and evolution; Sue Colledge and James Conolly, *The Origins and Spread of Domestic Plants in Southwest Asia and Europe* (2007), collects original articles on early agriculture in those regions. John E. Staller, Robert H. Tyko, and Bruce F. Benz (eds.), *Histories of Maize: Multidisciplinary Approaches to the Prehistory, Linguistics, Biogeography, Domestication, and Evolution of Maize* (2006), compiles the best available information on Zea mays.

Mabel Ping-Hua Lee, *The Economic History of China* (1921, reprinted 1969), is a history of Chinese agriculture with emphasis on soil depletion; Ping-Ti-Ho, *Studies on the Population of China, 1368–1953* (1959, reprinted 1967), is a scholarly study of population growth and of interacting variables, such as migrations, land utilization and tenure, and food-production techniques; Ifran Habib, *The Agrarian System of Mughal India (1556–1707)* (1963), is an informative text that covers cultivation techniques, crops, land tenure, village communities, and revenue administration; and Andrew M. Watson, *Agricultural Innovation in the Early Islamic World* (1983), is a systematic, informative overview.

There are a number of older studies of agriculture that remain relevant today. G.E. Fussell, *Farming Technique from Prehistoric to Modern Times* (1966), is a general review of the history of agricultural tools and techniques; David Grigg, *The Dynamics of Agricultural Change* (1982), is a survey of historical sources. Fritz M. Heichelheim, *An Ancient Economic History*, rev. ed., 3 vol. (1958–70; originally published in German, 1938), contains extensive and detailed information on ancient agriculture. Georges Duby, *Rural Economy and Country Life in the Medieval West* (1968, reprinted 1976; originally published in French, 1962), is a classic work on agriculture from the 9th to the 15th century. Also useful are Robert Latouche, *The Birth of Western Economy*, 2nd ed. (1967, reprinted 1981; originally published in French, 1956); B.H. Slicher Van Bath, *The Agrarian History of Western Europe*, ad 500–1850 (1963; originally published in Dutch, 1960); and Marc Bloch, *French Rural History* (1966; originally published in French, 1952–56). Jerome Blum (ed.), *Our Forgotten Past: Seven Centuries of Life on the Land* (1982), is a well-illustrated collection of essays; and Lord Ernle (Rowland D. Prothero), *English Farming Past and Present*, 6th ed. (1961), is a classic work describing six centuries of British agriculture. Also important is Cesare Longobardi, *Land-Reclamation in Italy*, trans. from the Italian (1936, reprinted 1975).

Works that address the advent of mechanized agriculture in Europe and the Americas include Reynold M. Wik, *Steam Power on the American Farm* (1953, reprinted 1959); Eric Van Young, *Hacienda and Market in Eighteenth-Century Mexico: The Rural Economy of the Guadalajara Region, 1675–1820* (1981); Clark C. Spence, *God Speed the Plow: The Coming of Steam Cultivation to Great Britain* (1960); and Ronald H. Clark, *The Development of the English Traction Engine* (1960). *Committee on Assessing Crop Yield: Site-Specific Farming, Information Systems, and Research Opportunities, National Research Council, Precision Agriculture in the 21st Century: Geospatial and Information Technologies in Crop Management* (1997), examines the use of technologies such as satellite photography and multispectral imaging in contemporary agricultural practices.

Hubert Martin, *The Scientific Principles of Crop Protection*, 7th ed. (1983), is a classic work by the world's leading authority on pesticides. George Ordish, *Untaken Harvest: Man's Loss of Crops from Pest, Weed and Disease; An Introductory Study* (1951), describes the economics of plant losses and their control; and Kenneth Mellanby, *Farming and Wildlife* (1981), studies the effects of modern farming on native flora and fauna. Theodore Saloutos, *The American Farmer and the New Deal* (1982), which explores U.S. agricultural policies during the first half of the 20th century, is an informative complement to E. Wesley F. Peterson, *A Billion Dollars A Day: The Economics and Politics of Agricultural Subsidies* (2009), which examines the problems of subsidized agriculture in the early 21st century.

INDEX